How to Get Married After Forty

A RADICAL APPROACH TO FINDING AND KEEPING YOUR MATE

THE PATH OF AUTHENTICITY

by

Karen McChrystal, M.A., MFCC

and

Steven L. Ross, M.A., LMFT

with Linda Riebel, PHD

Warm Springs Press

Tucson, Arizona

HOW TO GET MARRIED AFTER FORTY:
A RADICAL APPROACH TO FINDING AND KEEPING YOUR MATE

ISBN: 9780997384222

Warm Springs Press
Tucson, Arizona

Printed in the United States of America.

Contents

CONTENTS

Acknowledgments

Thanks to the many people who've helped us produce this book. Thanks for editing to Rob Christi, Linda Riebel, Laura Torbett, Juleen Ross and most especially to Ken Debono, whose publishing advice was also invaluable. Thanks also to the many teachers who've helped us formulate our ideas, including psychologist Richard Riemer, for his years of case consultation, to Hal Sampson and Joe Weiss for their pioneering work in the theory of the intelligence of the unconscious mind and the role of guilt in inhibiting our development, and to the late Midge Wood for her astute mentorship in the art of psychotherapy. We also wish to acknowledge all the clients who have enough trust in us as psychotherapists to reveal to us their innermost psychological motivations, thus further educating us in the ways of human nature. We have been richly blessed by all the friends who have been so real and present for us, and this has heartened and heightened our quest to make the world a more welcoming place by helping us all become the authentically loving beings we all really are.

Prologue

People of all ages need and want meaningful connection with each other. The search for a thoughtful, loving, and caring partner, an ideal mate, is perhaps the most poignant and compelling example of this universal longing.

Since everyone seeks love, we're writing for all readers, but especially for those over 40. We, the authors, were over 40 when we first sat down to write this book. Although our lives may be complicated by the time we reach middle age, we've seen in ourselves and in our peers a divergence of energies and priorities away from the hormone-driven, youthful abandon and/or focus on child rearing, toward something relatively simple and far less dramatic: finding friends, companions, and partners who are kind, caring, thoughtful, loving, capable of intimacy, and who understand and love who we really are. We want someone who is genuine, someone real. It may be that we always sought these qualities in our relationships, but after 40, this is what really counts, especially when it comes to romance.

This book is about finding and keeping a life partner. We have developed an "inside-out" approach, with seven steps to help you reach the cherished goal, marriage or otherwise. This approach is based on our years of counseling both couples and individuals. Practical steps are offered for overcoming the ten imaginary dangers of intimacy and for communicating honestly and completely.

We discuss how our unconscious mind works as our ally to help us find what we need for individuation (emerging from our family system and becoming separate, independent individuals in our own right), the foundational step for well-being in the adult world. Intimate relationships are our most potent crucible for this. Our experience confirms that it is not so much finding our ideal mate as it is becoming an ideal mate, and thereby attracting to us those with whom we have mutual recognition and respect, who complement our qualities with theirs, and who provide the most likely potential life-partners.

Those of us in mid-life or beyond might feel jaded after modest success and numerous disappointments or losses. But there is no need to be cynical. To gain insight and increase the chances of a happier life is always a worthy goal. Once on this path, we will attract others who are also on it. As we become more transparent and aligned with our core values, we can be "seen" by potential partners who are looking for these very qualities, who share these values and who therefore can appreciate and experience us fully. Graced by such companions, trust grows, making true intimacy possible.

Meeting people who might be an ideal mate seems more difficult the older we get. "The good ones are all taken," we might tell ourselves. Statistically, this just isn't true. People come out of first marriages and are again available. And some have been waiting just for you! If we are clear and completely aligned with our own intentions – for example to meet, find, and maintain another, or perhaps the first wonderful relationship, even later in life, our authenticity (rather than our pheromones) exerts a strong magnetic attraction, broadcasting who we are. It's not a spin, a strategy, or a "brand." It's who we really are.

Opportunities are everywhere. When you are around people, in gatherings, at an art opening, standing in line at the grocery store, or having a morning cup of coffee at the local café, don't automatically squelch that impulse to initiate conversation, to say something, anything, even out loud to yourself, when the thought strikes you. Maybe it's better if it's something positive, warm, or funny, but anything will do, as long as it's really you, really yours.

For example, let's say you're standing in line at the market and someone behind you has far fewer items. You say, "Oh, you have only a few items, why not go ahead." That is an opening, not necessarily for the person you are talking to, but for anyone within ear shot who may have noticed you but didn't see a way in.

Here's another example (true story): Say you are a woman shopping in the produce section of the supermarket. You see some imported produce and comment aloud – to yourself, mind you – "Oh my, these came all the way from Israel." Then a man you hadn't even noticed, but who had noticed you and was standing nearby, answers you and strikes up a conversation.

We're advocating authenticity at all times, but especially in the active (or passive) search for relationship. We can practice being real, authentic, not put-on, not disingenuous. If, for example, we write a personal ad full of euphemisms, subterfuges, and false notes, we may very well get responses, but the interest will be for someone other than who we really are. How long will it take for interested parties to figure that out? Then what? Better – and far more effective considering the potential it unlocks – is to be true to who we really are in the first place.

This integration, this full alignment of our inner and outer self into one attractive, coherent whole, is what we call "getting real," following the path of authenticity. It's certainly akin to a spiritual path, and we include exercises in Chapter 4 to help grow qualities like compassion and forgiveness, and to facilitate letting go of our attachment to controlling everything. If you walk this path with us, you will learn to more deeply appreciate, accept, and turn up the volume on who you are, explore and fine-tune what you really want, and learn concrete steps to ensure you get it. We all have within us the wherewithal to resolve the sometimes formidable obstacles and challenges inherent in this journey, moving toward freedom from forces deep within ourselves – unconscious beliefs and conditioning formed during our early years – that hold us back and sabotage our best efforts for personal fulfillment.

Only by being authentic, not through strategies, do we find who we are and who we're meant to be with. Finding and keeping a mate, we believe, both depend on authenticity. Authentic communication not only helps us "fit the lock" as far as finding the right person, it also optimizes our chances of keeping our mate.

More often than not, clear, authentic communication keeps bringing us back to the good reasons we initially had for wanting to be with a certain person. In some cases, it may clarify when differences have genuinely become irreconcilable, and then people can divorce or separate amicably, without carrying pain and baggage with them (which can mar the process of finding a more suitable mate, or damage the next relationship).

We have written this book for you, and the insights offered should prove valuable to finding and improving any intimate or close relationship you may have or want. Even if you sometimes feel discouraged, don't give up hope. Press on, undaunted.

~Karen McChrystal & Steve Ross, March 2016

1. The Gifts of Maturity

Forty-something, or older, and single! It's hard for unmarried people over forty to know if we're failures or late bloomers, over-the-hill or seasoned, jaded or wise, sad or just weary.

We're always the single one in a group of coupled-up friends, and friends add to the pressure by insisting that we just go out and meet someone. It's hard to avoid a lurking sense of shame about being single or divorced after forty, as though somehow we've failed. We may wonder if there's something wrong with us or if we don't have what it takes. We wonder if it's too late to find a life partner.

The penalties for being single are numerous. If we go to a vacation resort by ourselves we feel out of place among romantic lovers; when we go to the airport, we lug our own bags and watch cozy couples kissing each other "hello" and "good-bye"; we have roommates (at our age!); there's no one to share our intimate thoughts with; and the realm of unmarried sex isn't the playland it used to be. Going out looking in meat market singles dances or on blind dates can leave us feeling depressed, worse than if we'd spent our evening alone. We endure solitary breakfasts; there's no one to rub our back; no one to take care of us when we're sick. No one would even know if we choked to death at home on a piece of steak. There's no one else to take the dog to the vet or the VCR in for repairs; there's no one to congratulate us on landing a new account. And what we do alone in bed after surfing through T.V. channels leaves us with a feeling of emptiness.

We may feel on the outside looking in, as though we're the last single people left and no one wants us. We long to share our lives with someone, to build a commitment that lasts. To be without the intimacy we want is to live with an ache that can't be cured by drugs, diversions or dalliance.

The good news is, it's never too late to marry or to remarry. Being single or divorced over forty doesn't imply some fundamental character flaw or personality deficiency. People unmarried in mid-life may be more on course than they think. We can think of ourselves as late bloomers rather than failures. This is both because we may have lacked tools to unlock our gifts of self and because we took more time to develop our individuality.

Many of us haven't known how to communicate who we are. And we don't want to compromise ourselves. This book offers tools for truly meaningful connection, for bringing your accumulated wealth of experience to fruition in joyful, committed, and successful partnering.

Clients tell us many stories of being on the verge of giving up, deciding to stop playing games and just be themselves, and suddenly they find the person who really loves them for who they are. Our experience has convinced us that the best way to find the person you're meant to be with is to be utterly yourself. One woman told us,

> What I wanted in a man was someone who would be for me what I was willing to be for him, but I didn't really believe it possible. When I was ready to give up, I stopped trying so hard, and this man I really like appeared in my life. I think it happened because I stopped trying to be what I thought men wanted. I'm just myself, and that's what he was attracted to.

A DIFFERENT KIND OF RELATIONSHIP

Later marriages tend to be different from those made in one's twenties. Successful relationships that start when the partners are over forty have a quality of ease. People we know who've gotten married (or remarried) later in life, including ourselves, found their mates once they'd washed their hands of the old style of relating. Nearly all had had earlier relationships full of drama and painful struggle to work things out, hot sex and romantic fantasies, ups and downs, dramatic cycles of separation and reconciliation, agonizing over whether or not to settle for this or that relationship and wondering if it was too much to ask for more.

In the past we may have suffered through suspense, anxiety and discord. But these are not prerequisites for happiness. The no pain, no gain rule doesn't apply to relationships. It's Nature's way of saying, "Do something different!" Now it's as though we, the baby boom generation, have passed through our stormy period.

We've developed new partnering skills and can create relationships with genuinely compatible people.

Now we understand that to find our mates, there are two things to do: first, believe it is possible. Second, agree to conduct the search with a new set of rules.

Closing the door to stress and anxiety, we open another – the door to comfort instead of conflict, communion instead of competition. We need partners with whom we share a sense of homecoming – the feeling we're at last coming into focus. We're right to prefer this, and we deserve it! We've paid our dues. If the water isn't safe and friendly, we have no obligation to dive in.

One couple we know said their new relationship gave them comfort they had never known before. Life together felt peaceful, even when they had things to sort out. When we asked them what was different this time around, they said now they could finally relax and stop being anxious about whether or not this one would last. They had developed enough self-confidence to realize that even if it didn't work out, the next one would be better. It wasn't worth trying to make it work if they weren't a good fit.

Happy couples who've come together after forty can talk about everything with each other. There's no need to censor oneself in order to avoid upsetting one's partner. There's no worrying about the time not being right to express what one needs or wants. All the cards get put on the table in a conscious attempt to be completely in-the-moment authentic. These couples have learned to avoid the vicious cycle of judging, distancing, rejecting and blaming. They don't confine or entrap each other. They know it's O.K. to not always have electrifying or even frequent sex, but to be comfortable with the ebb and flow of sexual desire.

These couples wondered at first if their relationship was real – they were so different, without all the drama and uncertainty. What had happened? Partly they'd reached maturity, and gained wisdom from earlier experiences. They'd learned communication skills. Partly they'd gotten tired of the old business – they didn't have the energy to waste any more, and they now felt the effort for fleeting satisfactions and momentary victories wasn't really worth it. And part of it had to do with the focus of maturity shifting toward psychological and spiritual satisfaction, and away from the hectic dance of youth.

THE LESSONS OF LOVE

Learning to love is no small task. It is the ripe fruit to be harvested from maturity. The poet Rilke saw it that way:

> Young people, who are beginners in everything, are not yet capable of love: it is something they must learn. With their whole being, with all their forces, gathered around their solitary, anxious, upward-beating hearts, they must learn to love.

> Loving does not at first mean merging, surrendering, and uniting with another person – for what would a union be of two people who are unclarified, unfinished? It is a high inducement for the individual to ripen, to become

something in himself for the sake of another person; it is a great, demanding claim on him, something that chooses him and calls him to vast distances. Merging and surrendering and every kind of communion is not for them (who must still, for a long, long time, save and gather themselves); it is the ultimate, is perhaps that for which human lives are as yet barely large enough.[1]

Psychotherapist Carl Jung also believed the second half of life involves different concerns than the first. In early adulthood we're concerned with childrearing, cutting a figure in the world, measuring ourselves by our usefulness and by external reflections of our worth. And this carries a lifestyle with its own love style.[2]

Our psychological motivations are not so clear when we're young. We believe we want someone to make us happy or who will be the person we can't be, or whom we aspire to be. But in the second half of life we're more able to make ourselves happy and more able to be the person we want to be, instead of needing someone else to be that person for us. We focus inward, to illuminate the self that has been such a long time in the making, leaving behind games and blind motivations. The pull to do what is socially accepted and expected has less power over us, and we look deeper to find psychological and spiritual satisfaction.

It's no accident that many of us no longer have tolerance for games and postures, for pretending to be someone we're not. We deeply long for relationships we can relax into and be ourselves.

What keeps us from this is primarily our fear of being ourselves. Although we may be tired of the games, we may also have a hard time looking at who we really are and being authentic with others. We're afraid that if we reveal our real selves, we'll be unacceptable, used, abandoned, or that we'll be too needy or too threatening. In some cases we may not even be sure what our real self is – we lost track somewhere along the line as we had to adopt strategies and wear masks to survive.

To navigate the river of relationship without resorting to old, accustomed maps, games, strategies and disguises is a frightening prospect. We've become so familiar with the disguises and defenses learned over the years, they seem like old friends. But they deceive us. To give them up takes courage, and we need to replace them with something more reliable. To have the relationship we really want, we need to be fully ourselves, and that involves deliberately sailing into uncharted territory.

To begin, let's look at the models and maps most of us had to learn from, provided by our first teachers: our parents. Parenting is an extremely demanding job. The full nurturance and care of a young child requires psychological maturity which is rarely acquired before the age of thirty, and most of our parents started families in their twenties. In this light, we can see why they may have had little to offer us beyond physical well-being, if that. The psychological models they offered might have been an improvement over what they learned from their parents, but they were far from perfect and left us with gaps in our knowledge.

IN OUR PARENTS' SHADOW

In our parents' generation, social roles were more proscribed. While our parents generally did the best they could, we can build upon their knowledge to find ways more suited to our own happiness. We have the benefit of hindsight to understand that our potential as human beings is more than what our parents imagined for themselves or for us.

The roles they enacted have many positive aspects, but some aspects are unnecessarily limiting. For example, in our parents' generation, the martyred mother was typical – the woman who couldn't name her own needs or feel entitled to psychological support from her mate. These martyred women used altruistic self-sacrifice or controlling manipulations to get what they couldn't ask for directly. Or they may have tried to extract attention from unresponsive husbands by using illness, hysteria, complaints or silent suffering to induce guilt. Often they demanded attention and loyalty from their children when they couldn't get it from their spouses.

The martyred mother was generally married to another stereotype, the authoritarian or emotionally absent husband, who'd been brought up only to fill the role of breadwinner. These roles were often so limited or rigid that the marriage quickly became hollow. But the pain, anger and dissatisfaction this induced were seldom, if ever, addressed directly and resolved. These emotions were either hidden or were acted out in explosive, dramatic or self-destructive ways such as fits of rage, dramatic scenes, overeating or drinking alcohol.

So as children many of us not only had no models of healthy relationships, we were also preoccupied with our own psychological (or physical) survival or with how to help the family itself survive. In such an atmosphere we had little or no safe space to experience being who we were or to feel acknowledged and validated for it.

Given how vulnerable and impressionable we are in childhood and given the less-than-perfect role modeling most of us had, it's no wonder that we avoid intimacy. It's not that we don't want it, but we have a confused sense of it. Even if we try mightily to have something different from what our parents had, we somehow seem to end up with it all over again.

As a result, we enter adulthood caught between two equally unhappy alternatives: our unfettered energy and drives fight against the pseudo-stability of a dead or dying marriage. Negotiating that dilemma is no easy task. Over time, as we realized the magic of chemistry alone was no basis for a lasting relationship, and as we became aware of the dysfunction in our own and so many other families, many of us responded to that revelation with a pendulum swing to the other side: we choose caution and distance over the perils of yet another repeat performance. But now we have enough experience to understand how both these strategies thwart our true desires and needs. We can take a stand for what we really want, and what's more, get it! Given the proper tools, so gracefully offered by many great teachers of the humanistic tradition (such as Carl Rogers, Abraham Maslow, Rollo May, and Virginia Satir) and become the person we were meant to be, eventually connecting with a partner who loves us precisely for who we are.

The result for many of us has been that not being close seems the safest route. But we have enough experience now to understand how this thwarts our true desires and needs. We can take a stand for what we really want, and what's more, get it!

We, the authors, married in our early forties, and that's a large part of what motivates our writing. Our relationships have been successful in the ways we've described later-in-life relationships can be. We and our partners insisted from the beginning on physical and emotional safety, honesty and authenticity. To be more specific, when we feel emotional distance between ourselves and our spouse, we check in, usually to find that issues have gotten clouded or buried and it's time to do some emotional housecleaning.

Sometimes it takes time and effort to get behind the emotional blockade and reestablish a loving connection. We work at it until we're satisfied we've gotten to the truth of the matter. We never sleep on an upset. The effort it takes to resolve things more than pays off in the excitement of continuing to feel close to, and intimate with, our beloved. The encouragement we get from our partners to not let little things slip by – hurt feelings, dissatisfactions, irritations – keeps us going on the path of authenticity. To this do we attribute, above all, the great happiness that has characterized our marriages.

2. Ten Beliefs That Destroy Intimacy

What is common among many, including those of us over forty, which prevents satisfying intimacy are the *hidden beliefs* which keep us from being ourselves. This obstacle, fortunately, is surmountable.

Self-denigrating and self-limiting beliefs are formed early in life and remain at the root of what makes us feel bad about ourselves. If we're still alone despite reasonable opportunities, or if we get into relationships that follow the same pattern of failure over and over, we're probably harboring hidden self-limiting beliefs.

These beliefs reveal themselves in our "self-talk," a one-sided conversation we hold in our own minds. We have approximately 50,000 thoughts a day. If we kept a record of every thought we had, we'd likely discover a surprisingly large percentage of judgments, sarcasm, self-limiting and belittling comments which we took to heart and came to believe. After years of hearing negative comments, we internalize them, taking over for our parents (or whomever it was that delivered those messages) and telling ourselves the same lies, over and over. It feels right. It feels comfortable. No matter how dysfunctional and downright false they are, these dictums are part of the family system.

To maintain them – and we want to be clear about this, it is not conscious, it is an unconscious process – is to maintain the family bond, be a loyal son or daughter. Nothing is more important to a child for its very survival, no matter how crazy the family, and these beliefs are firmly anchored by fear and guilt as to what might happen were our parents to abandon us (or we them). Children's thinking skills are not adequately developed to counter unfair, irrational and neurotic reactions.

People hearing about trauma-based unconscious beliefs for the first time are often incredulous. How could this be true? Could it really be that bad? Why isn't it more obvious? Perhaps we are so steeped in these experiences as to be numbed by them, no longer able to recognize unfair treatment as something astonishing and reprehensible.

Dr. Joseph Weiss, whose insights about unconscious mental functioning have been so important to us in writing this book, explains in his writings about Control Mastery Theory that the primary motive behind children developing a sense of guilt in the first place, is tied to how dependent we are on our parents for protection. For example, if we perceive that our parent gets angry, upset or depressed because of something we did – or think we did – this belief (usually wrong) causes tremendous guilt. In other words, because we are so completely dependent on our parents, we worry about them and any possible disruption to our relationship with them. Children have magical thinking. They think they are responsible for just about everything that happens to them. We need assurances growing up that things that happen to our loved ones are not our fault. If we feel we caused our parents pain or suffering (feelings of being too powerful), or failed to alleviate any pain and suffering we see in them (feelings of being too weak), we feel guilty and try to repair the damage in any which way, including self-condemnation and self-punishment.[3]

Without skillful parenting, we are constantly caught in the middle of this really difficult dilemma. "Indeed," says Dr. Weiss, "the most profound and powerful feelings of guilt...may be rooted in a person's pathogenic belief that he has, in one way or another, hurt a parent.[4]

> For example, a child may infer (correctly or not) that any motive or behavior may threaten his all-important ties to his parents. One child may infer that if he is clinging and dependent on his parents he will please them; another child, that if he is clinging and dependent on his parents he will drain them; or the same child may infer both ideas. Another child may infer that he must be a bad boy in order to make his parents feel morally superior, or he may assume that he must be bad to protect an unhappy sibling whom the parents, because of worry, wish to perceive as good. As another example, a child may infer that by competing with a parent he will provoke the parent into a dangerous competition with him. Another child may infer that by competing with a parent he will provoke the parent to reject him, whereas still another child may infer that he must be competitive with his worried parents to assure them that they have not crushed his independence. generosity and even love toward him or her.[5]

The adults we become may still have those radioactive seeds broadcasting their toxic messages from a very deep place.

These internalized messages, deriving from those hidden beliefs, act as disguised commands. Were we told we were "boring," the less sterling sibling, not the brightest bulb in the chandelier? Were we identified or classified or shamed into thinking we were ugly or a failure? Thus will we remain, until awareness and acceptance of the imperfect system which produced and molded us, break the spell. Even being overweight can play a role in a dysfunctional family system and we may carry on, maintaining that weight to help maintain the system, long after the actual survival value is exhausted. It's unconscious. It's just in there.

As adults, if we continue telling ourselves, "I'm too fat (ugly, a failure, etc.)," we'll feel bad about ourselves, be unable to shine, and our potential partner will see that we don't shine and lose interest.

That's why there's wisdom in the idea that "it takes a village to raise a child." Somehow, we've got to develop perspective to get out of the vicious circle of old self-fulfilling prophecies, and relationships can be most helpful for doing this.

Groucho Marx once exemplified this kind of self talk when he said he wouldn't want to join any club that wanted him as a member. When we tell ourselves through our self-talk we're not fit to be in a relationship with someone we like and who's interested in us, we'll act accordingly and limit our opportunities.

When we know who we are and show up to the world that way, we attract people who can see and appreciate us. We need to get rid of old conditioning that keeps us from being ourselves. In this chapter we'll take a closer look at the hidden beliefs which underlie defensive relationship styles and learn how to dismantle them.

BELIEFS AND SELF-ESTEEM

Our defensive, self-limiting beliefs had emotional and psychological survival value during childhood. We've seen time and again how we are on "auto-pilot" and restrict ourselves according to those hidden beliefs about what we deserve, how we're going to be treated and what we have to do in order to survive and get what we need and deserve.

According to the American Psychological Association, more than two-thirds of children in the sampled community groups had experienced at least one seriously traumatic event by age 16.[6] "Traumatic events" include a broad range of experiences, such as abuse of all kinds, domestic violence, community and school violence, medical trauma, motor vehicle accidents, acts of terrorism, war experiences, natural and human-made disasters, suicides, and other traumatic losses. So it is safe to say that by age 16, most of us have been traumatized *more* than once.

Today, as adults with radically different agendas from those of childhood, these beliefs usually remain unevaluated, invisible and detrimental to our health and happiness. We can't be open and available for intimacy until we dismantle them. To examine outmoded beliefs and free ourselves to be fully present is the most important thing we will ever do. All else follows from how well we can do this in order to become more fully present.

These beliefs are held in place by a child's fear and guilt about what might happen if their parents abandon them (or if the child "abandons" the parent by being disloyal). Today, as adults with radically different agendas from those of childhood, these beliefs usually remain unevaluated, invisible and detrimental to our health and happiness. We can't be open and available for intimacy until we dismantle them. To examine outmoded beliefs and free ourselves to be fully present is the most important thing we will ever do. All else follows from how well we can do this in order to become more fully present.

We begin with a look at how early experiences mold our self concept and self worth. As children, our self-evaluation depends on the messages we internalize about who we are. The first messages come from our parents. According to one child psychologist,

> When a parent says, "What a good girl you are, the child gains an impression of herself as being a "good girl," no matter how undefined this impression may be. She brings these words inside herself, or internalizes them. When the parent says, "You are pretty, lovable, smart, sweet" and so on, the child gradually collects these positive words inside to form a view of self, together with feelings, stimulated by smiles, cheerful and warm voices, approving nods, and physical sensations, hugs, hand-holding, stroking a hurt ... But if the child experiences only negative feedback, neglect and rejection,

that child will automatically begin life with a sense of unworthiness. His thinking skills are not adequately developed to counter unfair, irrational and neurotic reactions to him. *Even though responses of significant others may not be based in reality, the child will accept them as truth.*[7] [italics authors']

Children are by nature altruistic and will try to do and be whatever they think they need to, to stay connected to and help their caregivers. The negative messages we receive from parents and other significant adults are often as wrong-headed and inappropriate as our misunderstandings of life at that age, and over time they consolidate into negative beliefs that go deep, become habitual and unconscious. Because of that, our later efforts at self-discovery and relationship are often a process more of inference than sequential, logical thought. Changes more often than not happen all by themselves, when we feel emotionally safe enough with trusted others to experiment (usually also unconsciously) with new behavior and hopefully find that it succeeds. As neuroscientist Daniela Schiller of the Mt. Sinai School of Medicine told Nature.com, responding to recent research at Northwestern University in Evanston, IL, "We used to think you need awareness and conscious understanding of your emotional responses in order to change them." But as a French psychiatrist quoted by Thomas Hora, MD, in his book, *The Soundless Music of Life*, said, *"ne guerit pas en se souvenant, mais on se souvient en guerissant,"* which translates: "We do not get healed by remembering the past, but we remember the past in the course of getting healed."[8]

THE GAUNTLET OF CHILDHOOD

Although parents love their children and do the best they can to nurture and protect them, even the best parents are fallible. Between failures of empathy and errors in judgment, few of us had families which could be called fully functional. In the worst cases, our parents were often drunk or abusive. Dysfunctionality seems to be the norm. According to international substance abuse and mental health expert, Terry Gorski,

> If you are among the millions of Americans struggling to get love right, the odds are you came from a dysfunctional family. In fact in the United States today, more people come from dysfunctional families than healthy families. It is estimated that approximately 70 to 80 percent come from dysfunctional families. Consequently, being normal in the United States today has very little to do with being emotionally healthy.[9]

Most of us need half a lifetime to recover from childhood. This doesn't mean we didn't get good things too. But we need to heal the pain and trauma if we want to experience our full potential as human beings. Intimate relationships can be a vehicle for our healing if we recognize their usefulness as such.

We need to look at our formative experiences to understand the root causes of what inhibits us in adulthood. A childhood full of danger and trauma will have kept us busy surviving psychologically if not physically, and will have left us a legacy of fearful beliefs about the world and our place in it.

As we have seen, if we grow up in chaotic, alcoholic, violent, or hysterical environments, it takes all our energy to orient ourselves to what's going on, keep our balance and devise roles and strategies to get us through. This deprives us of the stability in which to develop a rhythm of approach. Later in life, this shows up as not knowing when to approach and when to retreat. In the midst of this confusion, in the space between approach and retreat, we erect barriers and smoke screens to give us time to sort things out. The effect, however, is to keep us from having satisfying connections with others. We remain confused until we learn to recreate safety for ourselves, one step at a time and one day at a time.

We may have had all we could do to compensate for what was lacking in our parents' ability to parent. We'd have had little chance to explore who we were and what we wanted for ourselves. If, for example, we grew up with parents who weren't there for us physically or emotionally, we may have felt responsible for minding the store and been burdened by the weight of this responsibility. We might have formed the belief that if we weren't in control, the world would fall apart.

If we *were* neglected, exploited, abused or abandoned, we'd have tried to explain to ourselves why this should have happened to us. As children, we put two and two together, get five, and believe that bad things happened to us because we're bad people, don't deserve better, or have no right to be supported or cared for.

If our parents were burdened, needy or depressed they may have used us to make them happy vicariously. We felt pressured to live for them, to be there for them, to not ask anything of them, or even to make them look good. If we acted like separate individuals or tried to honor our own feelings, thoughts, needs and desires, we risked being labeled selfish or troublesome. We might have been punished or rejected for this or made to feel guilty for abandoning them or letting them down.[10] We might have formed a belief to explain this experience to ourselves, that if we ask anything for ourselves or try to live according to our own agenda, we're selfish and we hurt others.

What alerts us to our hidden, self-limiting beliefs are repetitive patterns of relationship that don't work. We may have spent the first half of life picking partners who seemed compellingly attractive, but who turned into someone totally different once we got to know them. Or we may have picked good partners but sabotaged the relationship just when things were going well. And some of us decided that, judging from our past experience, not being close was probably the safest way to go after all.

Our beliefs are hard to see because they're hidden from our conscious awareness. But once we recognize them, we can start the process of leaving them behind in order to find or create the relationship our heart desires.

AVAILABILITY

The easiest way to avoid responsibility for our lives is to blame others. A common refrain is, "no one's there for me." But if we've been looking and not found anyone, it's not because appropriate people aren't available. There are plenty of ways and places to meet eligible singles. The problem lies in our own degree of willingness to be available and in relationship.

You may have read about studies concluding that women over forty have a better chance of being killed by a terrorist than of finding a mate,[11] due to the overabundance of single women over forty and the preference of single males over forty for younger women. Looking into the so-called research leading to these discouraging conclusions, journalist Susan Faludi found it was based on faulty sampling methods.[12] The media got hold of the results and repeated what was initially a joke. The comment was repeated often enough that it took on the air of fact (much as our own mistaken childhood beliefs become facts in our adult lives).

Our chances of meeting someone go up dramatically if we actively set out to do it. Plenty of single women are simply too timid or too fearful even to look.[13] And there is a large population of men who become available after their first marriages end. The reality is there are plenty of eligible singles of either sex, and we can find a mate if we commit ourselves fully to doing so.

The most important factor is being ready to be close. In working with people looking for Mr. or Ms. Right, we've found the claim "no one's there for me" is really a cover for fear or unwillingness to be in an intimate relationship. To understand how willing you are to be in relationship right now, here's an exercise you can do:

Sit quietly and comfortably and close your eyes. Take a few moments to bring your awareness inside, and let the distractions of the day fade away. It may take five, ten or twenty minutes. Allow yourself this time. You can consider this your mental health break for the day.

After the distractions have quieted to a minimum, visualize or get a sense (not everyone is visual) of Mr. or Ms. Right standing before you, ready to get acquainted. Get as clear a sense or picture as you can. Now notice what you do. Do you appreciate how attractive and appropriate s/he is? Do you discount him/her? Do you make eye contact? How does he or she regard you? Invitingly? Rejectingly or disapprovingly? Play out the scenario as far as you care to, noticing your attitudes and reactions. Then come back to present time.

Now you have a lot of information about your own willingness to be with your ideal partner. Is the light green or red? If red, what stops you? If green, what draws you?

After we've seen our inner willingness or lack thereof, we can test it out in real life. What do we do in situations where we might meet a potential partner?

The poet Archibald Macleish said there is only one thing more powerful than learning from experience, and that is not learning from experience.[14] We all know this, but our blind spots cause us to repeat the same futile relationship patterns over and over. We say to ourselves, "I'll never do that again," and before we know it, we're repeating ourselves. Something more than meets the eye must be at work.

Hidden beliefs set limits to our achievement potential years ago. And now, still, it's as though we have a speed guard on our inner accelerator. As soon as we reach our designated limit, say fifty-five miles per hour, a buzzer goes off and we stop accelerating. Each of us has his own pre-arranged limit, except for the few among us who were encouraged and supported to take wing and fly. The story of Nicole illustrates how this works:

* * *

Nicole was fifty-two when she started psychotherapy. Despite a frustrating thirty-year marriage to a rigid, needy man who could meet very few of her needs, she always managed to rise to the occasion and be there for him. In fact, she never left him. He died three years before we met her. She'd gone through a period of grief and had come out the other side realizing she'd been a virtual prisoner during her marriage. Now she looked forward to a new life, new relationships and the possibility of remarriage.

Her difficulty was that she kept getting involved with opinionated, inflexible men with plenty of problems, just like her late husband. Around these men she became meek and compliant and couldn't ask for what she wanted or needed. Each man thought she was a great listener and loved how she took care of him – he was happy as a clam. At first Nicole felt needed and happy. Then she'd begin to feel obligated, suffocated and helpless. It scared her and she would then break off the relationship. After three such experiences she got depressed about her prospects for a better future, and this brought her into therapy.

Since we know early childhood experience is a source of self-limiting beliefs, we wanted to know about her upbringing.

Nicole's father had been a successful, generous, congenial man afflicted with rheumatoid arthritis since his mid-twenties. As his disease progressed, he became increasingly demanding and short-tempered, a change which young Nicole noticed but couldn't understand. On an unconscious level, she, like most children, felt somehow responsible.

Her mother was a schoolteacher and the disciplinarian of the house. She retired from teaching early and dedicated her life to taking care of her bed-ridden husband. This dedication and self-sacrifice made a strong impression on Nicole.

As we listened to Nicole's history, we thought about which unconscious beliefs might be at work to keep her stuck. To an already overworked mother, a child's needs are a burden, so the little girl may have decided not to express her needs. Perhaps this accounted for Nicole's self-sacrificing attitude. A little girl could believe that if she also sacrificed in her own relationship, she'd somehow be sharing her mother's burden. She might also harbor a belief that her mother would be hurt or upset if Nicole fared better in love than her mother had.

We shared these ideas with Nicole. The next week she came into our office looking more relaxed that we'd ever seen her. She'd remembered a traumatic incident that happened when she was eight years old, and this memory, although painful, relieved some of her anxiety. One Sunday her mother had insisted she wear a certain dress to her aunt's birthday party. Nicole hated that particular dress. However, since her aunt had given it to her, her mother was adamant. Usually an obedient child, Nicole lost her temper. Her mother got angry, sent her to her room, and then within earshot of Nicole behind the closed door, telephoned the aunt and said, "Nicole won't be coming to the party. She's been a bad girl and I'm sending her away."

We were appalled by this story and asked Nicole how it had made her feel. Nicole said,

> I had been very angry, but when I heard those words, I got scared. I remember feeling helpless and alone. I couldn't even run to my father because he was sick and in no position to help. I curled up on my bed and cried. Then I changed into my best clothes, packed my overnight bag, and sat on the edge of the bed, waiting to be taken away.

"Do you think she really meant it?" we asked.

Nicole replied,

> I did at first. It scared me. I couldn't stand that dress and it was worth it to argue with her, but it wasn't worth getting sent away! That was a terrible feeling, and it really upset me to remember it. Now I know she had no intention of sending me anywhere. It was just her way of punishing me for arguing and wanting to do things my way. This may sound strange, but it's as if I hear my mother's voice in my head, saying 'Do as you're told,' or 'Don't be selfish' – something like that.

Nicole realized she'd developed the belief – and what young child in her situation wouldn't? – that her martyred mother's burden would be eased if Nicole also suffered by not getting her own needs met. Conversely, she also believed she'd be a burden to her mother if she asserted herself and asked that her needs be met. These beliefs weren't literally true, but that's how her young mind interpreted reality. These beliefs then went underground. She wasn't aware until now that she had them, yet they'd been influencing her all her adult life.

One belief Nicole was conscious of was that men were needy and should be helped. This arose from her father's condition and her mother's response to it. As her mother had said to her, Nicole now said to herself, of the men she dated, "It would be selfish to worry about yourself now. This man needs your help."

Realizing old beliefs were influencing her adult life, Nicole began to monitor her behavior and self-talk. What she discovered was that she often set aside her own needs. Once aware of this dynamic, she began to assert her right to have her needs met. To her surprise, she began attracting more independent and attentive men. Her mother's voice accusing her of selfishness gradually receded into the background. Nicole still heard it, but much less often. When she did, she could identify it. She told herself, "This is my mother's voice and my mother's problem. It's not mine. I'm not really helping either of my parents if I limit my own chances for happiness."

THE TEN BELIEFS THAT DESTROY INTIMACY

We categorize ten grim, limiting beliefs that many of us carry into adulthood. (Lewis Engel, Ph. D., boils these down to only six basic imaginary crimes: Outdoing, Burdening, Love Theft, Abandonment, Disloyalty and Basic Badness).[15] These beliefs, while they're imaginary, cause us guilt or shame. Following are the ten beliefs:

1. I'LL LOSE MYSELF

2. I'LL BE HURT

3. I'LL HAVE TO HURT OR REJECT SOMEONE

4. I'LL LOSE CONTROL

5. I'LL BE SUCCESSFUL – AND THAT'S DANGEROUS

6. I'LL BE SUCCESSFUL – AT SOMEONE ELSE'S EXPENSE

7. I'LL FEEL FEELINGS

8. I'M TOO NEEDY/SELFISH

9. I'M A FRAUD

10. I DON'T DESERVE GOOD THINGS

* * *

1. I'LL LOSE MYSELF

This is the belief that if we get into a relationship we'll have to change our lifestyle and give up our freedom, indirectly threatening our sense of self. As one client, whose partner was unhappy with him, put it, "If I have to change my core beliefs, will I still know who I am?"

Here are the ways some of the people we have worked with expressed the fear of losing oneself to gain a relationship, a belief we call "I'll Lose Myself."

"Even my sister and my son say I'm selfish and vain for trying to develop an exercise plan."

"If I reveal my innermost thoughts and feelings, he won't like it..."

"If I show how vulnerable I feel, she'll take off..."

"My parents made it clear, do what they want or 'else'..."

When asked to complete this sentence, "If I am truly myself and act accordingly, I'll..." we have heard responses like this:

...hurt and lose my family and be alone and lonely.

...lose my acquaintances.

...lose self-respect.

...become destitute.

At the same time, people also saw a possibility of more positive outcomes:

…be less afraid.

…be able to stop trying to meet another's expectations.

…could be a true soul-mate to someone.

…be clear on what I want to do and how to do it.

…feel less anxious.

…be happier and have more energy and zest for life.

Carla had been single for three years since her last long-term relationship. What she said was that each time she dated someone she lost interest after the second or third date. She was getting really tired of this routine, and she wondered if all the good men had been taken. We asked her about her last serious relationship. Here's what she told us:

The man I lived with for two years, Ron, was so sweet at first. He did everything for me he thought I wanted. He even mowed the lawn and took out the trash without being asked. I didn't know why I felt so unhappy after the thrill of the first few months living together wore off. 'Here is a man,' I told myself, 'who would do anything for me. He's always bringing me presents, taking me out to dinner, finding little things to do for me, like bringing me breakfast in bed. Who could ask for more?

One day, I started asking for more, believing Ron wanted to be giving. I asked if he'd take a Sunday to go with me to a flower show, something I adore, but which doesn't particularly interest him. He hit the roof. I couldn't imagine why. He said, 'you're so selfish. I'm always doing things for you – all the time! And you want more. How can you be so ungrateful?'

I wondered about it myself, but then thought about all the things I never asked for. Before I moved in with Ron, I'd done a lot of things on my own, like playing tennis and singing in the choir, but I'd given them up to be with Ron because he just wasn't interested. I tried to get interested in everything he was doing, but frankly, television ball games bore me, and I don't like fishing or playing water polo – the things Ron loves. I tried my best, but then after a while, I let him go off with the guys to do his thing.

But I didn't feel I could go back to my old activities. The one time I'd gone to play tennis with my old tennis partner, Ron made a big stink. It was a week-end, and I'd spent the entire morning at the tennis courts. When I came home, Ron was fuming. He demanded to know why I'd been away so long. He expected me to do the housework and have his lunch ready for him. My feeling of elation from doing something I loved changed into guilt and entrapment. Being a housewife was not my idea of a fulfilling life.

After that, since I couldn't stand Ron being angry with me, and because if I'd stood up to him he might have left, I gave in and did it his way. I did what Ron wanted and tried to forget about my old life. I was in relationship now. Didn't that mean I had to make adjustments?

Finally, I couldn't stand it anymore. I tried to tell Ron what I felt but he wouldn't hear it. So I left him, deciding it would be better to live alone. That way I could do what I wanted, when I wanted, and have relationships just for hugs, dinners and sex. But it doesn't work. I'm getting tired of being alone.

***

We told Carla that a man like Ron, who required her to give up her own interests, wasn't interested in her happiness. Then we pointed out how she'd swung from one extreme to another. From playing the martyr for Ron, she'd swung to the other side and become too rigid in protecting her individuality. "There are men," we told her, "who want women with a strong sense of themselves, who'll stand up for what they want in a relationship."

Carla asked, "Then why haven't I met any? All the men I know are wimpy or macho." We replied,

You don't believe it's possible to be with someone who wants a strong woman, so you choose the other kind. Why not experiment with being yourself, completely authentic, on dates, and see what happens?"Carla agreed to try, although she was skeptical. And the thought of possible rejection made her anxious.

Happily, she called us after a few months and said she was having fun being completely herself on dates. She loved it, and the men who couldn't take the heat didn't call again. She started dating a man who was her equal. His name was Jack. He loved that Carla had a life of her own. He also insisted she do what made her happy, as long as she stayed connected with him and was fully present when they were together. Carla felt more peaceful and happy with Jack than with anyone else she'd known.

A few months after that, Carla called us again to tell us she and Jack had decided to live together. She said the secret to their success as a couple was that they not only shared common ground but also valued each other's differences and felt enriched each time one or the other brought home a tale of some delicious or intriguing experience they'd had or gave a whole new perspective on something they were discussing or considering. Because each of them took responsibility for their individual aliveness and happiness, they each brought something special to the couple.

When we abandon ourselves – what we really think, feel and want – we feel trapped, suffocated, or that our self is getting lost. If you've felt this way in the past, check to see if you were with a person who couldn't tolerate you being yourself. Did you downplay your opinions, wants or needs to make it more comfortable for him or her?

* * *

Healthy, satisfying relationships require some adjustment, but they don't demand burdensome compromises that aren't in our best interest. Some compromises are in the best interest of our relationship, however. For example, if your partner wanted you to visit her parents and you had other plans, consider what action would best serve the relationship. That is what's really in your best interest too. If you'd be happier as a couple if you stayed home, stay home. If you'd be happier as a couple paying a visit to the parents, do that. Seeing the bigger picture changes one's perspective and can prevent resentment. Resentment signals you're giving up something you shouldn't. In any case, such situations – common as they are – need to be talked about and explored together.

* * *

In another example, Erica and Sam had gotten caught up in the roles of in-charge-Mom and needy little boy. The more organized and take-charge Erica was, the more irresponsible Sam became. This triggered Erica's anger and, feeling contemptuous, she took even greater control. His response was to act even more childish, and on it went. Even when Erica identified the behavior she was caught up in, it was hard for her to give it up.

Then she remembered that as a child she'd gotten all her sense of value from being the "good child" who took care of everything, including worrying about her parents' needs. She thought about what it would feel like not to play this role and realized she'd feel like a scared little girl.

We advised her to reveal to Sam her scared, uncared for feelings and to tell him ways she'd like to feel looked after. Erica agreed to try. When she did, much to her surprise, Sam rose to the occasion. He liked feeling valued, needed and called upon to show his love. Erica had stopped pressuring Sam to play the role of needy little boy, the role he'd played in his family. When Erica stopped playing "Mom," Sam had the emotional space and acceptance he needed to act like the grown man he really was. He was only too glad to have a clear description of what Erica wanted from him.

And now Erica could get in touch with parts of herself she'd hidden behind her mom role and be real. Thus the spell was broken: they could both be authentic, and it worked!

***

Resentment is poisonous. The problem deepens if we allow it to build and we lose track of what originally caused it. It's very important to express any feeling of hesitation or unwillingness we have, the closer to the time of its occurrence the better. There's a simple effective technique to do this, using a special form of "I-statements," which we will describe in Chapter 4.

2. I'LL BE HURT AGAIN

Usually by the age of forty we've been deeply hurt emotionally, at least once. Each time it happens, we close up, like a sea anemone when it's poked with a stick by a curious beachcomber. If we remain closed, however, we don't get a chance to heal. What heals is being touched in a loving way, physically, emotionally or spiritually. Only in a relationship where we feel emotionally safe can we heal the old wound. This is because in the context of safety we have the emotional wherewithal to tolerate feeling the old pain, to sort it through and let it go.

In other words, we use unconscious assessments of danger and safety to regulate our experience of certain uncomfortable or threatening feelings. The more threatening the feeling, the greater our need for emotional safety. This important insight was brought to our attention by Drs. Harold Sampson and Joseph Weiss:

A person watching a movie about a love story experienced little or no emotion when the lovers quarreled and left each other. However, he was moved to tears when they resolved their difficulties and were reunited. He became happy, experienced a brief but not unpleasant sense of sadness, and wept.

To explain the moviegoer's paradoxical behavior (crying at the happy ending), I assumed that he identified unconsciously with one of the lovers, so that when the lovers separated, he was in danger of feeling sad, not only for the lovers, but also for himself. He felt endangered, however slightly, by the sadness, and so intensified his defenses against it. (He certainly did not repress his sadness deeply. He merely suppressed or isolated it.) Later, when the lovers were reunited at the happy ending, the moviegoer became happy, both for the lover with whom he identified and for himself. He no longer had reason to feel sad, and so was no longer threatened by the sadness which he had previously warded off. He decided unconsciously that he could safely experience the sadness and so lifted the defenses opposing it and brought it forth. He made it fully conscious, not for gratification, as the experience of sadness is not gratifying, but to gain relief from the effort he had been making to keep it warded off.[16]

When we don't have emotional safety in our important relationships, we'll stay emotionally defended out of necessity, though it may not be a conscious decision. This protects us, but also shields us from needed healing.

The more we're conscious of this process, the more effectively we can defend ourselves. We can choose to stay away from hurtful situations and insensitive or exploitive people. We don't have to be involved in destructive situations. This requires us to stand up for what we want and need.

Of course, people do hurt each other, intentionally or not. We can't rule out everyone as being potentially hurtful. Under normal circumstances, we can say, "Stop! It's not O.K. for you to treat me this way." Or we put up the wall temporarily, until we feel safe again. If the person doesn't respond, we walk away. This is what is known as a flexible defense system, one we can use in specific situations as needed, so we don't have to close down permanently.

Andrea was fond of falling in love. She'd developed an addiction to the wonderful feeling of letting go and walking on clouds for a couple of weeks until the crash. She couldn't hold back the enormous affection she had in her heart, and she loved to give unreservedly. But when she fell, she fell hard and got hurt every time. It wasn't that the men she picked were bad partners; they were just more reserved and cautious than she. Her unbridled enthusiasm prevented the development of any realistic sense of connectedness. The men were flattered by her attentions, but ultimately couldn't make sense of her professed adoration, got scared and withdrew, leaving Andrea alone and hurt, since she'd allowed herself to become completely vulnerable with no ability to pull back.

In one relationship she'd been so badly hurt she decided "never again!" But soon she began to want that old feeling of being in love again. Finally she met a man she thought was perfect. So she tried to love him. Surprisingly, and perhaps for the first time in her life, she couldn't. Her barriers had gone up. Her heart was closed.

In therapy she discovered fleeting, quasi-conscious fears that if she loved again she'd be hurt again. Then we discussed how in the past she'd leapt before looking and how she could change that pattern. It was important to her to know she could stay in control of how open she'd be and when.

To help her develop a way of regulating how quickly she got close, we gave her the following exercise:

Imagine your heart (with whatever image, sensation or feeling seems appropriate) opening a little, and then closing again. Then imagine it opening a little more, and closing. Experience your feeling of being in control of how much and when your heart opens. Continue with the exercise, opening your heart more and more, and being able to close it at will.

Next imagine yourself standing before the man with whom you want to be in love. Do the heart exercise in his presence, in your imagination, opening only as much as feels safe, and then close again. Do this exercise in your imagination until you feel ready to try it out in reality.

Andrea tried the exercise in her imagination for a few days and then tried it with Phil, her boyfriend. It was a new kind of feeling for her, to know she was in control over how close or distant she was. Then, she told us, she felt able to gauge more accurately whether or not she actually felt safe with Phil each step she took. When it didn't feel safe to go forward, she stayed put or retreated a bit, until she felt safe once again. Since she was no longer caught up in the headlong rush into giddy infatuation, she could keep her feet on the ground and allow the relationship to unfold in a natural progression. Phil responded in kind, taking some cues from her.

Andrea told us this felt comfortable and that she wished someone had taught her years ago that there was a way to create relationships slowly. She'd never known there was any alternative to the "Love at First Glance," Hollywood-style romance. Of course, she regretted a little having to let go of the "in love" feeling she'd grown so accustomed to. "But," she said,

...it's worth giving up that giddy feeling for being able to really know what I'm doing with someone. And I can protect myself from being hurt without having to stay out of relationships. I like going one step at a time. It feels grown-up, and also I feel a bit like a toddler, just learning how, to walk, one step at a time. In a way, I am a toddler, since I never learned how to do this before. And that's fine. Actually, it feels great!

This experience reminded Andrea of the time she wanted to climb a mountain. The path up the mountain wasn't really a path. Much of it was just rocks which had tumbled randomly down the slope. Each step of the way required her to test her foothold to be sure she'd found a solid one. If she went too quickly, she could easily step on a loose rock and have a bad fall.

At first, the climb seemed tedious, but after a while, she realized it was a valuable discipline. She couldn't rush or get ahead of herself. She had to make sure each step was safe. And she did get to the top.

3. I'LL HAVE TO HURT OR REJECT SOMEONE

We may have found that our efforts to stand up for ourselves as children met with discouraging reactions. We were given the impression these efforts were hurtful or wrong. So we may still believe that any time we say "no" or stand up for ourselves, we'll probably hurt someone's feelings.

Occasional hurt is inevitable in a relationship. Some people avoid relationships in order to avoid the problem altogether. But, for the most part, we exaggerate how much another person will be hurt by our self-assertive behavior. If we stand up for what we want, even when it means saying "no," telling someone what we don't like, or even that we want them to leave, they can usually handle it. How many of us have known someone who was truly devastated because of a rejection?

When we have to be rejecting, we can do it in a non-judgmental, non-punitive way. That means telling the truth about how we feel, kindly but bluntly. The "truth," when relating to feelings, is relative, but still critical. Feelings can change radically from moment to moment. They are still important to express because so much (behavior and assumptions, our own and those of others) is based on them. The truth may momentarily surprise someone or hurt their pride, but contrary to popular belief, truth doesn't cause damage, and rejection is not lethal. To be able to be rejecting is an essential skill in relationships. It allows us to define our boundaries and insures we don't waste our time or stay by default in an unhealthy relationship.

An example is the case where we think a person is nice but we don't have anything in common, so we don't want to pursue a relationship. However, since the person is so nice, we can't bear to hurt him by telling him we're not interested. Instead, we come up with excuses not to make time for him. Often enough that person takes the hint and stops calling. But what harm would being truthful in the beginning do? We could say, "John, I think you're awfully nice, but we don't have anything in common, so I'm not interested in pursuing this." Putting it this way would save John a lot of guesswork and suspense and keep you both from wasting precious time. And it's likely he'll handle it and be grateful for the frankness.

Sometimes we discover we need to leave relationship. It may be because we've outgrown it or finally discover it wasn't right for us in the first place. Whatever the reason, if we stay in it only to avoid hurting our partner's feelings, neither of us gets our needs met.

Some people try to set up a new relationship before leaving an old, hoping it will be easier to reject our earlier partner if we have the comfort of a new one in the wings. This seldom works. If we're still attached to our earlier partner, we won't be fully present with the new one.

We're better off closing one door before we open another, scary as that may sound. We may avoid being rejecting and linger in a bad relationship by rationalizing that what we have is better than nothing. Better-than-nothing relationships are nothing better than compromise, however.[17] Sometimes we have to push someone out of our lives because they won't leave otherwise. This takes more than simple self-assertion. We may have to say, "I don't like you" or "I want you to leave."

People have said to us, "She'll be devastated if I leave her!" Then we asked, "Really? How devastated?"

"She'll get very depressed and cry a lot," comes the reply.

And we ask, "then what?"

"She'll miss work and feel even more rotten."

"And then what?"

"Well, I guess she'll pick herself up and carry on. Probably she'll find someone else."

Being rejected is nowhere near as hurtful as being strung along by someone while that someone has secretly got one foot out the door, perhaps having an affair. The irony is that the secret is nearly always found out, causing immensely more pain to the one we're deceiving than if we'd been honest.

Even if the affair is never brought to light, the partner who is betrayed always senses, on some level, that something isn't right. S/he'll sense the relationship changing and know something's wrong. It's crazy making when you can't get confirmation or even discussion. The partner's denial arouses self-blame, but the person betrayed can't figure out how or why she's at fault. The fury that comes out when the truth is discovered can be damaging to everyone involved.

Of course, if the person we leave is actually suicidal, there's a serious problem. But rather than back down in the face of threats, it's better to help him or her get professional help. Otherwise we could be held for ransom for the rest of our lives. This form of blackmail does not make for a healthy relationship.

Whatever the situation, whether it's leaving a marriage or trying to tell someone he has bad breath, most people appreciate being told the truth. If we tell our partner, for example, exactly why we feel the relationship isn't working, s/he will feel respected enough to have been told the truth. And when this person understands why, s/he can deal with the situation on his or her own terms. The truth ultimately frees and empowers both parties to make good decisions and get more of what they want.

***

One client, Eddie, felt trapped in a relationship that wasn't giving him anything. But he'd stayed in it for ten years out of fear that his girlfriend, Rita, would get hysterical or commit suicide if he left. In talking with us, he admitted his life was going down the drain. He was disheartened by having to stay in the relationship, and he wasn't getting enough work because he was drinking a lot and missing appointments.

We asked what Rita was getting from the relationship. She'd been pretending that eventually Ed would be there for her and give her the love and the child she wanted. Ed and Rita had had endless discussions that went around and around, while they accused each other of not being what the other wanted. We helped them state clearly what they each wanted from the relationship. Through this process it became apparent to everyone save Rita that they were mismatched.

Ed summoned the courage to tell Rita he wanted out. Rita did get hysterical, threatened suicide and accused Ed of every possible kind of caddishness. But he held his ground and calmly (most of the time) repeated his case to Rita: he didn't love her and couldn't get what he wanted from their relationship, nor could he give her what she wanted.

After a couple more weeks of emotional turmoil, she got it. She saw she could no longer sway Ed by making scenes, and she accepted who he said he was. Then they were able to plan their separation with admirable cooperation.

4. I'LL LOSE CONTROL

People who need to feel in control of their intimate relationships believe something bad will happen if they give up control. They worry they'll be abused, abandoned or led astray, or they're afraid to confront feelings they don't know how to handle.

Betty was a bright, pretty woman you might think could have any man she wanted. But she always dated men who were weaker or less intelligent. She knew her choices precluded deep involvement, but staying in control was more important to her. She eventually discovered three dangers she unconsciously feared:

1. Acknowledging her anger. She was furious at her father. When Betty was a child, her father had been nursed by his wife back to health from a life-threatening illness. He then abandoned his wife for a younger woman, leaving his wife to fend for herself and young Betty. Betty carried into adulthood all the rage she'd felt at her father's treatment of her and her

mother. She now believed her old anger would overwhelm her if she allowed it to surface, so she kept it locked up.

2. Betty was afraid of being used and abandoned as her mother had been.

3. She believed that having a good relationship would make her mother feel bad by comparison.

As a result of these hidden beliefs, Betty chose weak and exploitive men, not expecting to find anyone different from her father. And she had to stay in control to avoid her mother's fate.

Once aware that she set up relationships based on hidden beliefs, she agreed to try something new. Soon she met Jim, who was strong and whom she couldn't control. He knew how to stand up for himself and seemed genuinely to care about her.

In the spirit of trying something new, she allowed herself to be gradually drawn into the relationship, despite the anxiety she felt at not being in control. Slowly she opened up as she began to trust that Jim wouldn't exploit or abandon her. He wanted her to stand up for herself and not cater to his needs at her expense. She was spared her mother's fate and so could become deeply involved. She realized in the process that holding herself back to not outdo her mother made no sense. It wouldn't help her mother and it would be too depriving for her. A few years later Betty and Jim were married.

5. I'LL BE SUCCESSFUL – AND THAT'S DANGEROUS

Couples sometimes sabotage perfectly good relationships. One reason is a sense of undeservingness, based in shame about oneself. There are two types of shame. Healthy shame tells us what we may and may not do as members of our society, preventing us from violating cultural or social values. Then there is pathological, toxic shame. Helen Block Lewis describes it this way:

> A person whose daily life is pervaded by feelings of worthlessness and inadequacy is one whom we would describe as "shame prone." A shame-prone person is often in a state of emotional distress and unable to function well in everyday life because of difficulty speaking, thinking, and interacting with others.[18]

Shame-prone people are in distress. They are painfully self-condemning, they feel worthless and disgraced, they have difficulty interacting socially and may want to hide or disappear completely. Lewis says they may even have difficulty speaking fluently and thinking coherently.

As John Bradshaw put it,

> Shame as a healthy human emotion can be transformed into shame as a state of being. As a state of being shame takes over one's whole identity. To have shame as an identity is to believe that one's being is flawed, that one is defective as a human being. Once shame is transformed into an identity, it becomes toxic and dehumanizing.[19]

Shame and guilt are related, but there are important differences. Shame has more to do with violating social norms than guilt, which arises primarily from internal conflicts such as a violation of one's own values. Shame arises when one's 'defects' are exposed to others, resulting in real or imagined criticism or judgment by others; guilt, on the other hand, comes from one's own negative self-evaluation.[20]

But the main point is that we may develop shame and feelings of undeservingness either from being treated badly when we're young, or from simply having parents who were ashamed of themselves, from whom we learn to feel ashamed, out of identification with them. When the child internalizes a sense of shame, this serves to severely inhibit the development of his or her own identity. If the childhood crises are not handled satisfactorily, the person continues to fight his early battles later in life. Many adults are still struggling to develop a sense of identity. Erikson optimistically claimed that it is never too late to resolve any of the crises,[21] however, even if a crisis is "resolved," later trauma may undo it.

The sense of shame can be painfully acute in persons who have been sexually molested, beaten, abandoned, humiliated, disgraced, dishonored, or told they were inadequate. In adult life, this translates into, "I don't deserve to have a good relationship" or "I don't deserve to be treated well." This belief can manifest later on in different forms. One client, who had grown up receiving very little positive feedback for his accomplishments, felt that nothing he did would ever be supported or celebrated, while another expressed discomfort receiving praise because she couldn't believe that any such positive feedback could be true.

For example, a woman who had grown up feeling emotionally abandoned, blamed for family problems, and had been repeatedly told she was a disappointment, had serious relationship problems as an adult. She always felt on tenuous ground: "When is the other shoe going to drop and you'll leave me?" She said at one point she started dating "stupid men" who were less likely to "see through me," with the hope that she could change them if she just "did it" right. She craved validation. She would test her boyfriends' loyalty by doing risky things to see if they would support her and stick with her. As you might imagine, the "other shoe" frequently dropped.

In an intimate relationship, one risks exposure. In a person who feels ashamed and undeserving, the fear of being exposed as essentially defective, irreparably and unspeakably bad,[22] is intensely magnified; and instead of proudly coming forward with who they really are, their tendency is to withdraw and hide.

In the context of an intimate relationship, toxic shame is a real challenge. Under the right circumstances, it can be overcome by coming out of hiding, honestly sharing our feelings with our significant other, and by seeing ourselves mirrored and echoed in the eyes of at least one non-shaming person. In severe cases, we would highly recommend counseling / psychotherapy or working a Twelve Step program. An accessible and thorough book about shame, with detailed steps for overcoming it, is John Bradshaw's *Healing the Shame That Binds You.*[23]

Bradshaw explains,

> Having developed a sense of self-worth, a person feels he is loveable and wants to love another. A person with a solid sense of self is capable of connecting with another in an intimate relationship. Intimacy requires vulnerability and a lack of defensiveness. Intimacy requires healthy shame. Most people have a way to go in terms of developing intimacy and connecting skills when they get married or enter a long-term relationship. But the great thing about a committed relationship is that the relationship itself is a form of therapy. If both partners are committed, most of their differences can be worked out and even appreciated.[24]

6. I'LL BE SUCCESSFUL – AT SOMEONE ELSE'S EXPENSE

Another reason couples often sabotage themselves is hidden guilt about having a better relationship than their parents or siblings. The belief is that our success will make someone else feel bad by comparison. We may generalize this fear of success to our professional life as well, holding ourselves back so we don't surpass others. People are usually incredulous when we first suggest that they inhibit themselves in order to not show up someone they care about. Logically, it makes no sense. Yet, when people inhibited for this reason take a second look at their lives, the recognition is practically unanimous. As one client put it, "I can see now that one reason I haven't found a better relationship is a weird anxiety about being happier than my parents." And a man who was having trouble as a consultant found himself unwilling to assert his expertise if he thought his client would see that as a "put down."

**

The case of Marti illustrates how this belief can influence our behavior for years, well into adulthood. Her mother, at the age of twenty-nine, had been an overwhelmed housewife married to a workaholic. She withdrew into her own world of anxiety, loneliness and desperation. Her young daughter, Marti, sensing her pain, responded on an unconscious level by "keeping her company" – by also being a loner and staying home with Mom. Marti's mom "appreciated" her daughter's sensitivity and everyone knew they were very close.

As a teenager, this child was anxious and isolated. Later as an adult she kept to herself, didn't trust men, either personally or professionally, and had difficulty with relationships in general. The hidden belief holding her back was that if she had a better life than her mom, her mom would feel abandoned and bad about herself.

* * *

The story of Sally and Joel offers another example of how this belief operates:

Sally was a high achiever and had good social skills. She climbed rapidly up the career ladder, and along the way fell in love with Joel, who cared deeply for her. She liked him enormously, and their romance went beautifully for several months.

Then Sally began making self-deprecating remarks in front of Joel. He told her she shouldn't undermine herself this way. As far as he was concerned, she was the tops. She soon started behaving in ways unconsciously designed to convince him of her unworthiness – she got drunk a few times and made a fool of herself in public, even though she was not in the habit of drinking. In restaurants, she clumsily spilled things. She showed up late for engagements with Joel. Finally one day, in Joel's presence, she flirted outrageously with another man. Her antics finally drove Joel away.

After he left, Sally couldn't believe what she'd done. Joel would have been the perfect husband for her. She cried over the telephone, begging him to come back, but it was too late.

Next she started behaving badly at work. She did things which made her look stupid, that were against her better judgment, and which eventually got her fired. At that point she came into therapy. We discovered that her mother had given up a promising career path to be a housewife. Keeping house bored her to tears. Furthermore, she'd married a man who didn't love her, just to have security. She was miserable. Sally felt so sorry for her mother she unconsciously decided to keep her company emotionally – the "misery loves company" idea we also saw in the story of Nicole.

Sally had made this decision when she was twelve years old. It became part of her hidden belief system and continued to influence her adult life. She acted as though success was dangerous.

* * *

Aaron's story is another example of how we impede our progress if we believe our success will hurt someone else. Aaron had never let himself become successful, although he was well-equipped to do so. He was a mild, eager-to-please, single forty-three-year-old man. Intense feelings of shame and incompetence brought him into therapy. These feelings depressed him and he felt dissatisfied with his life.

Aaron began by discussing how he felt totally incapable of fixing things around his house. He felt contempt toward himself because of it. He recounted how a loose front step had provided work for a local carpenter, and that leaky faucets always had their washers changed by a plumber. He didn't feel there was anything wrong with this *per se*. The problem was that although Aaron had written off his ability even to learn these things, he couldn't help feeling emasculated every time he had to call for help. He was caught in a vicious circle and got more and more depressed.

We thought we could learn something from Aaron's self-talk, so we asked him to monitor his thoughts whenever he faced a minor repair at home. He noticed how he told himself things like, "I can't do this. I'll probably break it," "I'm such a wimp," or "I'm a failure."

We'd been exploring these issues for a few months when Aaron remembered a painful childhood incident. He'd made a gift for his mother in his elementary school wood shop. While his creation reflected great enthusiasm and pleasure, it was far from perfect. Nevertheless he was very proud of it and with great excitement brought it home.

His mother was delighted, but his father criticized the piece, pointing out its imperfections. "Face it," said his father. "You're just not mechanically inclined. You're just like your mother." Aaron was hurt. He felt unfairly treated, but it never occurred to him that his father might be wrong. Although his mother didn't seem to mind her gift's imperfections, he took his father's words to heart.

As we talked about this memory, Aaron discovered he'd formed two beliefs as a result of this experience – beliefs that were now holding him back. The first belief was that he was manually incompetent. This belief stayed with him throughout adulthood and eroded his self-esteem. After all, men are supposed to be mechanically inclined, aren't they? To avoid the painful awareness of his apparent lack of mechanical abilities, he became a journalist, about as nonmechanical as you can get. But even in this career he hesitated to take on complex assignments because he doubted his ability.

His second belief came from his father's scornful comment, "You're just like your mother." This was a more sensitive issue which Aaron hadn't mentioned to us at first. He felt too inhibited to approach attractive women, believing he was sexually unappealing. This troubled Aaron deeply. He'd even begun to wonder about his sexual preference, although he'd never been sexually attracted to men.

Aaron recognized a connection between his lack of assertion with women and his need for his father's approval. As a child he'd believed that being unmanly (just like his mother) pleased his father. Whether he was right or not wasn't the issue. The result was that as an adult he unconsciously enacted his decision to limit himself in order to prove his father right. He unconsciously tried to protect his father, at the expense of his own self-esteem.

It's common for youngsters to feel responsible for their parents' problems. They often feel they should help ease the burden and mistakenly think that by limiting themselves they can accomplish this.

As adults we look back on these efforts and see how misguided they were. As children we have no such perspective. Aaron sensed, but couldn't conceptualize that he was trying to please his father and improve their relationship by acting small, weak and incompetent.

After remembering the wood shop incident and understanding how it had influenced him, Aaron felt greatly relieved. He could now recognize the harsh internalized voice of his father and choose to ignore it. This enabled him to replace his self-deprecating belief system with a healthier, more accurate one. Tentatively at first, but then with greater frequency, he began to connect with attractive women who found him attractive as well. At home he tried to fix things himself, and when he did call in a professional, he watched carefully, asked questions and learned.

Aaron had finally understood his part in his family drama and realized he didn't have to feel responsible for his father's unhappiness or feel guilty for getting on with his own life. He discovered that people found him more interesting when he didn't try to please them, but instead was himself, successful in his own right.

***

If you're the sort to sabotage a good thing, or if you know you're capable of more than you've already achieved, ask yourself if you believe there's something psychologically dangerous about being successful. To discover whether you feel guilty over having a better relationship than your parents, ask yourself if you feel sorry for them in any way. Do you feel sorry that they don't seem to be happy together? Do you imagine they'd feel bad if they knew you had a happier relationship? Would they merely give lip-service to being happy for you?

When you began dating, how did they react? What did they say about your dates?

Now, having this information, do you feel having a successful relationship would be like rubbing salt in their wounds? Or, alternatively, would your success have merely reminded them of their own unhappiness? In the latter case, do you imagine you should curtail your own success to protect them from being aware of their own problems?

Guilt, from violating (or at least believing we violated) our own (or our family's) values, is easy to acquire. We might feel guilty being successful if there were members of our family who couldn't be. If, for example, we have a parent or sibling affected by tragedy that limits his chances for success, or if someone in the family got the short end of the stick and can't be as successful as we are, we might secretly believe we have an unfair advantage. We may believe we got the love they should have had. Or we may reason, "How can I be happy when he had such trouble and misfortune?" This is, in a way, a kind of loving loyalty. But it doesn't really help our handicapped sibling or emotionally wounded parent. It just means there are two tragedies instead of one.

We can't help a less fortunate person by becoming unfortunate ourselves. Chances are our success will be an inspiration and example, not a hindrance or source of resentment.

It's not our responsibility to make another person happy by protecting him from the reality of life. Each person is responsible for how he feels about himself and what he does with his life.

7. I'LL FEEL FEELINGS

Some feelings are not pleasant. We dislike feelings such as anger, hurt, grief, abandonment, humiliation or confusion. But the only way to avoid them is to deaden ourselves. Then, instead, we feel bored, depressed or numb. The feeling vocabulary chart in Chapter 4 will help you determine how wide a range of feeling you allow yourself.

Fear of feeling is usually not conscious because our defense against feelings goes up so early, in life. When we experience painful, traumatic or overwhelming events in childhood we don't have the skills to handle them. Often, being in touch with them wouldn't have done us any good. So instead, we repress them, simply in order to survive emotionally. For example, if we felt tremendous anger as a child but weren't allowed to express it or if expressing it did nothing to change the situation, we may have disowned our anger and cut off our awareness of it. The anger may still be there, but we no longer experience it directly.

***

One client, Bill, told us he couldn't understand why he occasionally had murderous fantasies toward his girlfriend Lucy. There wasn't anything Lucy had done bad enough to merit Bill's wishing her dead.

In therapy, Bill discovered he was still angry at his mother. She'd turned to him for her primary emotional support, since his father wasn't emotionally available. Bill resented the obligation and was still angry about it. But he'd never told his mother because she acted hurt if ever he opposed her.

To make matters worse, if he did get angry, his father told him to take a hike, and that was the end of it. There was no way Bill could win by having his feelings. So he disowned his anger and turned down the volume on all his feelings in the process.

Now the anger was spilling over onto his relationship with Lucy, and Lucy wasn't even the real target! When all this came to light, we supported Bill in having his feelings. This made it safe for him to own his anger at his mother. We instructed him to envision telling her how he felt and then doing in his imagination anything he wanted. At first Bill was reluctant to even imagine angry action toward his mother.

Bill also wrote his mother a letter which he didn't send, telling her how angry he was. His murderous fantasies toward Lucy subsided, and he began to live more fully in touch with all of his feelings, including his anger, which now assumed appropriate proportions.

***

If we become intimate and vulnerable, inevitably unresolved feelings from the past will surface. We need to talk about these feelings so they don't spoil our relationship.

In short, we can reclaim our full range of feelings by allowing ourselves to feel them all, and then by noticing whether they're from the past, even if triggered by something in the present. Then we can identify what originally made us feel angry, depressed or bad about ourselves, or whatever it was. When we remember what really happened and feel the feelings we had at the time, we resolve the experience and we're finished with it. It's like fitting the last pieces into a jigsaw puzzle and then putting the puzzle away because the picture is completed. We're then free to live fully in the present.

But sometimes these negative feelings originate in what has become an unconscious thought or belief, resulting from earlier trauma, and thus a negative feeling may return unbidden from time to time. This signals us that there's another, deeper, layer of understanding we need concerning whatever event or cascade of events triggered and reinforced that particular negative feeling and the associated belief and accompanying thoughts. Very often, we first become aware of the immediately prior reinforcing event. Then later, an earlier precursor will trigger the feeling again, and we need to identify that earlier event. And so it goes... we work backwards until we finally get to the very first time we experienced the traumatizing event. So, in summary, if those negative feelings return, then you can notice them, identify the mistaken thought or belief attached to them, and replace them with the corrected and accurate thought, finally getting to the bottom of what caused it all in the first place.

8. I'M TOO NEEDY/SELFISH

When we become intimate with someone, we reawaken our desire for companionship, nourishment, closeness and acceptance. If we learned early on not to ask for anything, intimacy can be very uncomfortable. If we've been alone for a long time, our desires can seem overwhelming, and we'll believe we want too much.

However, it gets very simple if we're aware that what we're really asking for is someone to be there for us, not to do all for us. And we're entitled to that. Then our desires are not so overwhelming.

If we get involved with someone who's not ready for intimacy, we may believe it's our desires that are too much or that we're selfish. It's important to consider that it may be our partner who isn't present enough to accept the gift of self we offer. Some children are accused of being selfish any time they ask for something.

As adults, these people are so concerned about the danger of being selfish that they hold back ordinary statements of wishes, such as, "I would like to stay home and watch the TV show that I've been looking forward to all day."

It's easy to make this mistake if we were treated during childhood as though our desires were a burden. For example, a child may want nothing more than instructions about how to tie his shoelace. If his parent is already overwhelmed, she may react to her child's request as if it were the last straw and scream at her child, "You'll be the death of me!" The child puts two and two together and comes up with five: "When I ask Mom for help, I make her really angry, and I might make her die." The child then forms a belief that his needs are too much and could hurt someone. This gets reinforced over the years.

Kids are extremely empathic and altruistic and often want to help a burdened parent. In the child's mind this is enacted in a self-sacrificial manner, such as believing that not asking for anything will help. We may have concluded that it was our needs which burdened our parent. We can't easily grasp the idea that our parents have their own problems, may be unable to cope, and that this has nothing to do with us.

Sometimes we accurately perceived that there wasn't enough to go around, and we needed to do without. Perhaps our family was poor, or there wasn't enough time to give attention to everyone, either because there were too many people, or because parents were incapable of giving much emotionally.

Adults, under ordinary circumstances, don't really need that much emotionally. Basically, we want to feel listened to, understood, appreciated and cooperated with. This isn't asking so much! When we feel too needy or selfish is when we don't get even these basic needs met, or we worry it's too much to ask for that they be met.

Whatever the cause, we can test our fear of being too needy or selfish by asking our partner how he or she feels about us asking for something. Either he's happy to give or is busy or preoccupied. We're entitled to know the reason when we don't get what we ask for. We're entitled to reassurance, if we need it, that it's not because we don't deserve it or because our partner doesn't love us.

Sometimes our partners can't give to us because they're feeling resentful or angry. They may refuse to give as a way of punishing us. Then the issue of their original anger needs to be discussed. It may not even have been something we did, but something that happened in another context.

If we're the one withholding, we can say, "I don't feel like giving to you right now. I'm still angry about what happened earlier. Would you like to hear about it?" The partner who's withholding may not start this conversation, in which case, we have a right to ask why we're not being given to.

It's important to ask with an attitude of curiosity rather than demanding to know or accusing him or her of being withholding, tactics which are, guaranteed to make our partner feel angry and defensive.

Many people involved in political or social causes sacrifice their own interests because they have the hidden belief that satisfying their own needs contributes to the suffering of others. More often the truth is that if they took good care of themselves, they'd have much more to give to others. And since they'd feel good about having given to themselves, their self-esteem would be enhanced. The result would be increased energy, health and generosity.

9. I'M A FRAUD

Many people rarely had the experience, and so can't imagine they'd be loved for who they are. So they pretend to be someone they're not. Trying to be the person someone else wants them to be, they forget how lovable they are themselves. Intimacy would make them remember. But by now this is a scary prospect because they think who they really are can't be all that great. And if they're not as good as they thought they were, they sure don't want anyone else finding out! To keep from letting the cat out of the bag, they start believing their own pretense and conclude that it is their inner being which is false.

This belief is closely related to Belief #5: "I'll Be Successful and That's Dangerous." Both are based in toxic shame. Very often the person who has a deep sense of shame will have erected a false personality – a facade. And so they go through life feeling they are a fraud. As Bradshaw put it,

Toxic shame is unbearable and always necessitates a cover-up, a false self. Since one feels his true self is defective and flawed, one needs a false self that is not defective and flawed. Once one becomes a false self, one ceases to exist psychologically.[25]

But of course, the cover-up prevents there being any true intimacy.

* * *

A former yoga teacher came to us for therapy. He told us he'd traveled widely as a yoga teacher and was revered by students, seekers and well-wishers. He'd always given freely of his time, energy and knowledge and knew that people benefitted enormously by what he taught them. One day, however, he stood alone in his room looking at himself in the mirror. He was suddenly overcome with feelings of disgust and contempt. He told himself he was cheating the public and was unworthy of their high regard. Then he ripped the belt off his saffron-colored robe – both symbols of selfless service – and threw it at the mirror, cursing and feeling like a complete fraud. He hadn't broken any vow or disgraced himself in any way. But his feeling of worthlessness and fraudulence cut deep to the bone. For years he'd kept these feelings at bay through his rigorous spiritual practices. Eventually he could no longer hide from his feeling of fraudulence. So he left his order.

Once out of uniform, he found himself isolated and had difficulty forming intimate relationships. He eventually came to therapy to get help to be the person he wanted to be. He wanted to cast off his mask of asceticism and spiritual pride, alleviate his self-loathing, lead a normal life, and feel valuable as who he was.

The feeling of fraudulence is common among people whose social or professional role has forced them to suppress their own feelings and sense of self. Their willingness to suppress themselves developed early in life, when their upbringing caused them to believe their real self was not good enough. But the only thing we do that is really fraudulent is to lie about what we really think, feel and want – in short, to lie about who we really are.

10. I DON'T DESERVE GOOD THINGS

The belief that we don't deserve the good things comes from a childhood of deprivation, non-validation, or being constantly criticized. This treatment could have been psychological or physical. If we grew up with all the physical amenities we wanted or needed, we may have been seduced away from noticing if we weren't being given to emotionally. If a parent is emotionally withholding or reserved or doesn't actively express interest in his child's emotional well being, the child will feel rejected, by default. The adult's absence of affection and concern are interpreted by the child as a sign of his being unworthy of love. Because the child can't understand his parent's emotional limitation, he forms the belief that he doesn't deserve love.

This is a devastating belief, similar to the belief that if we ask for anything we're being selfish. In the latter case, we also believe our having anything for ourselves will take from someone else. Believing we're basically undeserving is different in that it doesn't matter whether or not some other person's welfare is at stake. Deprivation is the just reward for being basically unworthy.

The cure for this belief is to feel entitled to good treatment, and we can choose to feel this way. Why wouldn't we? Are we really bad people? Have we done terrible things? Most of us haven't done anything bad enough to warrant emotional or physical deprivation. We all want good things for ourselves. Having them enhances our self-esteem, which is essential to our ability to be a good partner. Jack Kornfield, a Vipassana meditation teacher, cites the Buddha's teaching that our bearing should be like that of a king or queen, prince or princess, out for a stroll, because that, spiritually speaking, is really who we are.

Not receiving positive feedback and being systematically criticized and blamed instead is traumatic and devastating. Sociologist Harry Stack Sullivan pointed out years ago that without feedback from others, we would have no idea who we were or even be able to maintain a consistent personality.[26] This does not bode well for children growing up in environments characterized by deprivation and trauma of various kinds, which can give rise to a serious pessimism. One person summed it up like this: "The glass is half-empty, with a hole in the bottom." Our clients have expressed the effect of these crippling experiences in painful ways:

> I think I was raised to feel like a second class citizen, unworthy of being a valued person whose thoughts and feelings mattered. That may be why I feel a void when I think about who is my true self.

If I did as I was supposed to, exactly right, things went smoothly enough. But if not, I felt shunned, rejected, run down every which way possible. Leaving on the light was like stabbing someone.

It was as if I was worthless and as good as dead. I have felt sad, lonely, and confused. I have felt threatened, inadequate, scared, and worthless. I am learning now to grieve.

We can neither overstate the importance of good parenting, nor minimize the terrible and life-long impact of a childhood without consistent, empathic connection with reliable loving, nurturing and protective caregivers.

SELF-TALK

Sometimes thoughts flicker so quickly through our minds we don't notice them. If we pay close attention to this stream of conscious-ness – often referred to as self-talk – we can uncover our hidden beliefs. Relationships, especially good ones, seem to unleash a torrent of them. When we get close to someone, we usually have automatic thoughts about why we shouldn't be vulnerable. If we don't catch the thoughts and stop them, they'll dictate our behavior.

To stop automatic negative self-talk, we need to first become aware that we're doing it. Pay close attention to the things you tell yourself and try to sort them out. See if you can recognize who told you these things about yourself. Our negative self evaluations have their roots in something a parent, childhood authority figure, relative, or close friend told us, once or (more often) repeatedly.

There may be some "John Doe" voices also, people who weren't close to us, but whose cutting remarks caught us at a vulnerable moment. You'd be surprised at the impact of such incidents. Here's an example of how a seemingly insignificant event in a child's life can have a deep and lasting hurtful impact:

> When Harry was in the fifth grade he had an argument with a girl classmate over who could play the record player first. The conflict became heated, and at the peak of their fuss, the little girl suddenly blurted out, with great feeling, "Oh, you're nothing but a fat, ugly little boy." Unbelievable as it is to the adult mind, Harry took this comment into himself, aided by the strong emotional charge of the situation, and accepted it as truth. From that time forward, he viewed himself as ugly and unattractive to girls. Even though he was usually seen as attractive by girls, at twenty he was still under the spell of his fifth grade classmate's assessment.[27]

Until we become aware of our hidden self-limiting beliefs, we'll be influenced by them. They act as filters on reality, influencing our choices and behavior.

AUTOBIOGRAPHY EXERCISE

When we become aware that we're making negative self-assessments, we can ask ourselves if we really believe we're so unworthy or undesirable. Instead of only marshalling evidence to prove the case against us, we can give equal time to the other side and marshal evidence on our behalf. A good way to counter negative self talk and marshal evidence in our favor is to write an autobiography, an account of the important things that happened to us up to the present time and how we feel about them. We can include any beliefs about ourselves we're aware of having formed at the time.

Start by looking back at your life and trying to remember the earliest time you had to make a choice that later seemed to turn out badly and is still not fully resolved. It could be the way you handled an argument with a friend, what courses you decided to take in school, your first disastrous love affair or any number of painful or awkward events that left lasting impressions. As you review your past, look also for the reasons you had at the time for making the choices you did. If you look closely, you'll see that under the circumstances you did the best you could have done. There were good reasons at the time for doing what you did and in the manner in which you did it.

If, at the time, you didn't exactly know why you did something, perhaps now, with some perspective, you can see more clearly. For example, one woman named June was in career transition and took secretarial jobs just to pay the bills. June was a highly educated person who deeply resented having to do what she considered "grunt" work for arrogant bosses, typing, taking dictation and filing. She thought her intelligence was being wasted on mindless tasks. But shortly thereafter she made another career change and became a journalist, and her ability to type very fast with no mistakes, which she'd learned as a secretary, was invaluable.

In your autobiography, include also your accomplishments, all the things you feel proud of. And account for how you did the best you could at the time with what wisdom you had. This will help you remember evidence of your worth. This retrospective view of your life will not only give you concrete evidence of your good intentions, innate wisdom and how you have always done the best you could have under the circumstances, but will also demonstrate to you that you learned something from every experience, which you needed in order to take the next step.

Now when you catch yourself thinking self-denigrating thoughts, you'll have evidence to counter your negative stories. By keeping track of the positive evidence of your worth, you can stand up to your worst enemy – your own self-judgment!

THE PERSON WE'RE MEANT TO BE

Parents usually give their children everything they can, and it's usually a rich mixture of behaviors, emotions, attitudes and expectations. Few of us as children have the skill to cull the good from this mixture without also internalizing the bad. As adults we can correct the past by consciously embracing the good resources we internalized and weeding out the negative or destructive influences.

This is the effort required in order to become distinct from our parents, to assert our real selves and to manifest the gifts which are unique to us. The process of doing this is called separation/individuation, in other words, developing into separate and unique individuals in our own right.

If the unborn butterfly in its chrysalis were helped by a kindly passerby who simply slit open the case, the butterfly would die. It needs to struggle against the confinement of its cocoon long enough to develop enough strength in its wings to fly.

The effort we make to become our own person is the effort to pay attention, to remain fully awake, to notice what we think and do. When we attend to our thoughts, we can, like Nicole and Aaron, separate our true self from that of our conditioning – the internalized voices of others and the stories and beliefs we made up in childhood. Then we can to act in our best interest by telling ourselves that which is true and affirming of who we are.

To find our life partner, we need to reclaim our real self, the one that went underground years ago. We need to pay attention to what we really think, feel and want, and to honor what's in our best interest. The more authentic we are with ourselves and with others, the more easily we'll attract partners who value our authenticity.

3. You Were Right to Wait

Many of us have good reasons for not being ready for marriage until after forty. But it may be hard to resist the pressures of cultural stereotypes and Hollywood notions of falling in love. Commitment isn't something that happens simply by meeting someone who knocks our socks off and after a time deciding we're going to make it work. Commitment is built step by step. We need to understand who the other person is, and vice versa. We need to be compatible on many levels, not just in our lifestyle.

COMMITMENT ISN'T A LEAP OF FAITH

Beverly is a single, bright, energetic forty-four-year-old. Each time her boyfriend of two years asked her to marry him, she was plagued by self-doubt and ambivalence, to the point of paralysis:

> He wants me to make a commitment. I don't feel comfortable with the idea, but maybe I should … Maybe I have commitophobia … Maybe I should take the leap … Normal people make commitments, don't they? If I don't make a commitment, he'll think I'm toying with him. Maybe I'm just using him. What if he turns out to be the wrong person?

Commitment isn't about leaps of faith. Commitment is what we're *left* with after all the objections and obstacles to being with someone have been worked through and cleared away. Commitment is the expression of a thorough understanding and acceptance of each other. This is very different from the popular notion that when you're in love you should throw caution to the wind and take the plunge. Unfortunately, people do this all the time, even people who should know better because they did the same thing the *last* time, and that didn't work either.

It's hard to go against the urge to merge when we're in a giddy rush of attraction, but apart from being a natural urge, sometimes the attraction is only Nature's way of getting us to finish unresolved issues from the past. The story of Corinne illustrates this point:

A forty-year-old single professional woman, Corinne spent her early adulthood jumping into relationships before she'd had a chance to understand what motivated her. By her late thirties she'd been so hurt following her misguided ideas about relationship and commitment that she wanted no more of the old business.

To celebrate her fortieth birthday, Corinne took a vacation by herself in the Caribbean. She was prepared to have a good time by herself, but what a perfect setting if she were to meet someone special! Being alone was starting to depress her.

She arrived full of anticipation. The first day she spent unwinding and soaking up the sun. For breakfast on her second day, she went to the local deli. The man working behind the counter had a great tan and a palpable animal magnetism. She figured he'd know where the best beaches were and asked him. Not only did he answer her question, he also asked her to join him for drinks that evening.

"Maybe," she said, thinking she might, but only if she had nothing better to do. After all, he worked in a deli and she was a professional. By the evening her curiosity had gotten the best of her as she wondered what it would be like to go out with someone so different from her. At least he could show her around. She went to meet him at the local open-air bar, where they listened to jazz and drank beer.

His name was Andy. His stories of how he survived without having to work too hard were hilarious. Corinne loved the story about his method for getting a free dinner: when a fishing boat came in, Andy and a buddy rowed out in a dinghy and held up *Playboy* magazines for the fishermen to see. The fishermen lowered the ladder for Andy and his friend, and in exchange for the skin magazines, included the two in their magnificent feast of bar-b-qued fresh fish.

Toward the end of the evening, returning from the ladies' room, Corinne noticed how Andy waited for her with his hands casually resting on his inner thighs, framing his rather large genitalia outlined in tight jeans. The effect was not lost on her. She was, after all, on vacation.

Andy and Corinne spent the ten days together. She felt comfortable with him and was powerfully sexually attracted. Whereas she usually intimidated men, Andy wasn't the least threatened by her. Corinne also found him the funniest men she'd ever met. Here was a guy, she thought, who's so creative he'll be able to keep up with me.

One evening while she, Andy and a friend of his were steaming fresh clams on the beach, Corinne began to shiver with cold. There weren't any extra coats or blankets and she couldn't get comfortable in the cool air. The two hardy men didn't feel the cold. Corinne complained. Andy whispered in her ear, "Handle it!" So Corinne handled it. And she got the feeling Andy knew how to handle her, which she liked.

She perceived Andy as having Buddha-like equanimity, which allowed her to be completely herself. She ignored the little red flags – such as when Andy asked her to pay for their expensive dinner out, for all of their drinks and for the clams they baked on the beach. She ignored how much marijuana he smoked and how much alcohol he drank. He could handle it, she thought. The tropical setting was so perfect and she felt so good, she decided her concerns were petty.

At the end of the ten days, they bade each other farewell. But once back on the mainland, Corinne couldn't get Andy off her mind. She called him, he called her, and so on, over the next couple of months. Although Corinne knew it would be risky to invite him to live with her, she thought the way to have commitment was to swallow her fear and go for it. She persuaded Andy, and he agreed to come move in a month later.

Once Andy arrived on Corinne's turf, he revealed another side of his personality. He turned out to be the most demanding man Corinne had ever known. He wanted constant attention. When Corinne got tired of giving it, Andy got depressed, drank beer and watched TV for days at a time. If they went out to meet her friends, Andy got stoned or drunk. If Corinne refused him favors, he got angry and punitive. If she objected or felt hurt by his anger, he treated her with contempt. Her feelings meant less than nothing to him. What had appeared to be Buddha-like equanimity on the beach turned out, in the new context, to be a callous indifference to anyone's needs but his own.

Corinne got more and more furious and finally, after he'd stolen various items from her, she threw the bum out.

Afterwards Corinne understood why her friends had from the beginning been unanimously skeptical about their relationship. No one had lost any time telling her they thought this relationship was all wrong. Only after she'd had enough of being used and treated callously did she realize she'd repeated one of her old patterns. For years she'd been picking men who, though clever or even brilliant, had hidden agendas of wanting to exploit women. While she intimidated most men, the ones she couldn't intimidate, she dated. Their brilliance and strength hid their inner neediness, and they used their brilliance the better to exploit Corinne.

Corinne later discovered that what she'd been drawn to all along was yet another version of her father. Since her father was charming, brilliant, handsome and somewhat authoritarian, she'd had a hard time understanding that on the inside he was so needy he'd had no room for her emotional needs when she was growing up. Instead he emotionally exploited her as a substitute for his alcoholic wife, Corinne's mother. The bond she'd felt with her father was based in her feeling valued because he needed her for emotional support. Similarly, Corinne had felt comfortable with Andy because the feeling with him was the same as that which she'd had with her father. Andy needed her emotionally the same way Corinne's father had needed her. He expected her to be there for him without his being there for her. Corinne mistook for love what was really only sexual attraction and the familiarity of an old pattern. Unconsciously she was motivated by an unresolved childhood need to get her emotional needs met by her father.

Corinne had unconsciously recreated her old drama so she could once and for all find her way out of her repetitive pattern. None of the re-creation had been conscious. Her unconscious mind had intelligently gotten her to set up the situation she needed to be able to finally understand, consciously, and to heal herself. This time she had recreated it in grand dimensions, but now could learn from the experience and consciously understand, emotionally as well as mentally, that she had to stop falling for people who couldn't give anything back to her.

Corinne's realizations didn't happen overnight, but after she understood what was going on and saw how to change the old pattern, she could resist the urge to repeat it. As long as she'd been under the spell of the past, she couldn't be with men unless they fit the old pattern. But now she was more present, emotionally available and determined not to ignore when she felt exploited as she had with Andy and the others before him. In this frame of mind, she met a different kind of man.

This new man was as right for her as Andy had been wrong. The new man treated her with consideration and respect, didn't leave her wondering where she stood, and was completely sincere. He was emotionally available and could see and appreciate who she really was. Because they felt safe to reveal themselves fully to each other, they were a match – as lovers, living, working and playing together. Because they each felt safe, they could talk about and work through their doubts and fears. After two years together they'd made a genuine commitment and were married.

In mature relationships, leaps of faith aren't required. Instead one gains a thorough knowledge of the other through a step-by-step process.

* * *

We've taken a lot of time telling Corinne's story because the lessons are pointed. Leaps of faith may be well-rationalized, as were Corinne's, but they are too often motivated by powerful unconscious beliefs. Corinne had three unconscious beliefs operating in her relationship with Andy: She believed she did not deserve good things; that if she asked for anything for herself, she'd be acting "too needy"; and that if she spoke up about what she really thought and felt, she might hurt Andy, given his hidden insecurity and neediness.

Genuine intimacy and commitment build only when our hidden beliefs can surface and be worked through.

CHOOSING A PARTNER

How do we know when we've met someone who will be good for us? Does it depend on how turned on we feel, how powerful the sexual attraction is? Is it because that person possesses all the icons of material happiness? Because he or she has qualities or achievements we admire or want to emulate? Because he has talents we wish we had?

Surface appearances can be misleading, as can sexual attraction. Even though sexual attraction is part of nature, and a romantic relationship without it doesn't really work, it can't be the only thing upon which we base our decisions. The person who turns us on the most is not necessarily right for us. A strong sexual attraction may result from unconscious motives, as in the case of Corinne. We can feel powerfully attracted to someone who re-awakens feelings we grew up with, feelings we had with our parents. These feelings are part of old patterns. They can be highly sexualized only because a child's bond with his parents is experienced in a kind of sexual way – not genitally, but as a physical basis for love. As adults we interpret this attraction sexually. But both the child and adult levels are operating at once, and sexual attraction can blind us to the adult dynamics which are the important ones to pay attention to.

If we get involved with a person we feel compellingly sexually attracted to, something important will always happen even if we don't find our life partner. At worst, and most often, we'll relive unfinished childhood dramas, have hot sex and learn a little more about ourselves. Once our lessons are learned, if there is little else to sustain the relationship, we need to move on.

People over forty like the zing and sizzle as much as anyone, but no longer rely on them as criteria for great relationships. Priorities change with experience and wisdom. Most of us want generous doses of honesty, compatibility and peace of mind along with good chemistry. It's a question of balance. We don't want to exhaust ourselves putting on a big athletic event or having to strategize, trying to impress and calculate the right moment to speak our minds and share our feelings. Can't we please be real?

As we mature, it's more interesting to be genuine, to stay in touch with our feelings, with what we really think and what's in our best interest. We don't want to live according to what others demand, although a good relationship is always a give-and-take and our mate might reasonably require certain things of us (and vice versa). Though possibly scary, being genuine is a great relief and so much easier than pretending to be someone we're not or saying "yes" when we mean "no."

GETTING THROUGH THE MAZE

Being real is like picking up the thread that leads us out of the maze, as did the mythic Greek hero, Theseus, who had major relationship difficulties. All the eligible women were being devoured by a monster who demanded yearly tribute of a living virgin. The monster lived in the middle of a labyrinth so complicated that no one, even if they escaped his jaws, could find their way out. Theseus went in with a ball of thread which he unraveled as he went. He met the monster, slew it and then followed the thread back out.

Early in life we enter the maze – a complicated web of obligation, expectation and entanglement. This becomes the basis for all our thinking, our fundamental paradigm.

When we're in our thirties or forties we concern ourselves with working our way out of the original paradigm. The thread which helps us find our way out is our inner, unconscious drive to rid ourselves of self-limiting, self-destructive beliefs and to live life to the fullest. Our old thinking and belief patterns are what stop us from being who we really are. To slay the monster of childhood fear and confusion we have to confront our old paradigm, our childhood structure of thinking, and consciously replace it. Picking up the thread is the choice to be as genuine and truthful as we possibly can.

WHERE TO BEGIN?

How do we begin? What criteria should we use in selecting potential partners? Accompanying our efforts to become internally prepared for a lasting relationship, we also need to pay attention to who interests us, even if we don't understand why we're interested. Interest is our clue there's something important about connecting with this person. Even if our interest is based on some unfulfilled childhood need, we need to go with it, if only to fulfill that need. And we may not know in the beginning what's really in store.

What about the "nice people" we may not be at all interested in but feel we should be? Not to worry. When the time is right, when our agenda shifts from completing the past to being fully in the present, we'll have as many chances as we need to connect with a nice person. If we're not interested now, we won't get much from relating to them.

Once we've identified who interests us, we need to pay close attention to our intuition or gut feeling about them. Gut feeling is literally in our gut. This is where intuition originates physically. Our gut will tell us if this person is safe or not to be trusted. We intuitively recognize danger signals, even if we ignore them. If our stomach gets tied into knots when we're around a certain person, that's a good sign s/he's not to be trusted. If we feel at ease, we can take the next step.

We'll notice varying degrees of comfort with different people. With one person we may feel nervous and worry we'll do something wrong. Another person will outwardly have all the "right stuff" – financial security, physical attractiveness, smooth talk – but for some reason, we feel bored. Sometimes boredom is a defense against opening up, due to some hidden fear, valid or invalid. But here we are talking about boredom as the signal that there's nothing in common, no juice, nothing to connect us meaningfully with that person. One person may seem very knowledgeable and interesting, but we'll have a feeling there's something hidden and it makes us uneasy.

We may even dismiss someone who's potentially a good mate, because it's too easy being with them. We feel relaxed, safe and interested, but it just couldn't be right. Even though we talk a blue streak, laugh and have a great time, we dismiss this person as a romantic interest because he's "not our type"; the packaging isn't quite right; he's going bald; she's a little overweight, perhaps not quite the right height, not blonde (brunette, or your type); his career is solid, but definitely not glamorous; and so on.

And what if the wild sexual rush is missing? We remember from the past what it was to lock eyes with someone across a crowded room and feel pulled headlong, out of control and loving it, into a living fantasy. Of course it can happen that way, but we tend to forget how short-lived these episodes often are, how messy, how we swore never to do *that* again. Now here in front of us may be Mr. or Ms. Right, but our thoughts wander and our eyes stray to other faces in the crowd.

Apart from the importance of sexual appeal, packaging is not the other half of the equation for a relationship to work. What makes it work is the experience of emotional safety. Only when we have safety can we be open and fully ourselves. Safety nurtures intimacy as well as healing and growth.

BEING SEPARATE

When we're true to ourselves and with a nurturing person or supportive group, we experience our distinct individuality and thus our difference from others. This is separateness, and along with individuation, it is a critical part of growing up and becoming our own person. People are afraid of separateness if they don't have a good sense of who they are as individuals or if they believe they wouldn't be appreciated or loved for who they really are. Some believe expressing differences will hurt their partner's feelings, but the steps to authenticity teach us that in healthy relationships, others welcome our uniqueness.

In relationship, separateness means continuing to have one's own life at the same time as sharing it. It means I can bring to the relationship my individual perspective, experience and wisdom, and my partner can do the same, without judgment, criticism, disdain, contempt, devaluing or attack of any kind. Some people believe being separate precludes intimacy. They worry that if they pursue interests or have opinions that differ from those of their partner, they'll grow apart. On the contrary, bringing our uniqueness to our relationship makes us more interesting to our partner. The richness of intimacy depends on bringing *all* of who we are into the relationship, rather than pretending to be alike.

Sometimes couples are alike in many ways, and completely opposite in many others. Maybe he's very down to earth; she's a mystic. He's very sensual; she's more mental. Their taste in food is opposite. Their taste in music is different. They like different amounts of social life – he enjoys lots of group activity and she prefers more solitude.

But on the other hand, there are plenty of things they both love doing together – hiking, bicycling, dining out, good movies and gatherings of good friends. They can agree that if one of them wanted to do something the other wasn't crazy about, it would be okay to make other arrangements. Rather than compromise or comply, they each could do what they liked to do. Sometimes this would mean doing things separately, which works better than being together doing something one of them doesn't really enjoy or can barely tolerate.

Perspectives on life can be different yet complimentary, and the glue between two mates can be not so much the activities they do together as the way their outlook on life meshes. For example, they can be quite matched in their senses of humor, their ethics and aesthetics.

Differences don't mean incompatibility, but sometimes one has to make an effort to translate different ways of seeing and thinking in order to be understood. In our relationship, for example, I tend to be conceptual and he more concrete and visual. What seems obvious to me sometimes isn't to him, and vice versa. We have to translate our different perspectives into the other's perceptual language. When he can't fathom something that's clear as day to me, I'm tempted to get impatient and assume he's falling asleep at the wheel or has a screw loose. We each have to resist becoming impatient and remember our perceptual styles are different.

Incompatibility occurs when one person has little respect for the other. A partner's behavior may be morally repugnant, self-destructive or abusive and cause us not to want to be close to them. This is qualitatively different from the areas of likes and dislikes, perspectives and talents.

Compatibility means feeling comfortable with another person, feeling emotionally safe and having sufficient attraction and interest to share daily life.

WHO WE'RE BECOMING

Relationships are a vehicle for our transformation and growth. As important as who our partner is today is who s/he is in potential, what s/he is capable of becoming. If we're basically compatible, and if we don't delude ourselves with wishful thinking, we can help bring out each other's potential. To assess someone's potential accurately, however, we need to regard him or her with respect. What our partner reveals to us in the moments he or she feels respected is who he or she really is. Once we see him or her clearly, we can treat them as that person all the time, even when his or her mask goes on again. Treating a person as the best person they're capable of being supports them to be that person and to work through old conditioning. If we hold our partner to his best in this way, we give the benefit of the doubt in the fullest sense.

Another example is a man I knew who hid behind a mask of toughness and intellect. He was so successful being tough and brilliant he made a good career as a prosecuting attorney. With his girlfriend he could occasionally be vulnerable. But he kept vulnerability to a minimum because he couldn't believe she'd like who he was on the inside. In his view, what was behind his facade seemed like what was behind a theater curtain, where all is dark. The action is all out on stage, in the bright lights, where people play their favorite roles.

His girlfriend kept expressing interest in who he was behind his toughness and brilliance, enough so he was drawn to look more closely at who he was on the inside. He began to reveal more of his feelings, what he really thought and felt when he wasn't acting the prosecuting attorney. To his surprise, he rediscovered a playfulness and innocence inside him which he hadn't been in touch with since childhood. Even more surprising to him was that his girlfriend liked this part best. Her appreciation of his inner self made it safe for him to reveal it more and more.

This experience enabled him to explore other interests and finally to realize there was another career path he could take. He'd secretly longed to change jobs, but hadn't been able to envision anything else he'd want to do. Now he thought he'd enjoy being a stage theater director. He'd become so fascinated by the difference between roles and the actors behind the roles, he wanted a career which would involve him in these issues. His willingness to be vulnerable with his partner had opened him to possibilities he'd never realized were there.

DETECTIVE WORK

Intimate relationships sometimes require psychological detective work to understand what the real issue or discord is about. For example, when an emotional response doesn't make sense, we can try to track its source. A likely place to start is with the subtle parental influence. Negative parental influence can be like a ghostly presence in our relationship and can wreak emotional havoc unless we become skilled at recognizing it. We can identify it by noticing when one or both partners consciously or unconsciously act like one of their parents. It's important to notice each time this happens. We do it by noticing changes in our behavior. Once we identify a behavior pattern that's more that of a parent than our own, we can stop it and get back to who we really are.

This writer's father was a frequent ghostly visitor in my marriage. His way with people had often been devaluing and patronizing, wrapped in some abstract philosophical point that one couldn't understand or relate to very well, not to mention argue against. This undermining influence was so subtle it was difficult to detect. Usually my partner and I wouldn't recognize it until I started feeling uncomfortable and knew something was wrong. I'd feel put down or devalued. This was unusual in our relationship, but so familiar from past experience that I had a hard time recognizing the pattern. The words my partner used were always quite refined, so it was hard to catch him acting like his father just from listening to his words. He might say something like, "I don't like how you view the world, but that doesn't mean I don't like you."

Well, my world view happens to include everything I do, so in my experience, it is a large part of me. I could get into a philosophical argument with him over whether or not we're just our essence or whether our selfhood includes how we view the world and what we do, but that gets hopelessly abstract. Angered and defensive, I'd ask for clarification.

"Why don't you like it?"

"It hasn't landed you a paying job, has it? How can it be any good?"

This comment would make me even angrier.

"How can you assume what I'm doing is no good when you don't even take time to find out what it is?"

Tempers would escalate. I'd be tempted to tell him his world view wasn't any better, but that would be *too* tit-for-tat, too childish. We wouldn't get anywhere at all until I'd finally identify what I was experiencing.

I'm feeling put down and hurt, I don't know what's going on, but it feels terrible and I feel really angry."

Having said that, I realized I *had* been put down by my husband's dismissal of my world view. Then I knew what I wanted.

"I want respect! And that means giving me the benefit of the doubt!"

He told me when he doesn't see results or know what's happening, he always assumes I'm doing something wrong. This statement horrified me. I couldn't believe he was saying this. It was totally out of character.

"Intelligent people give the benefit of the doubt, especially to their so-called beloved!" I said. "This must be your father talking. I can't believe the real you would think that way."

It takes time to know someone well enough to recognize parental patterns, and they usually take one by surprise. But it's one of the most important things we do to keep a relationship on track.

Sometimes we have the impression everything is on track, that we've finally finished with our parental issues. Although this could be the case, these are more likely only momentary respites, preludes to the next surfacing of unresolved issues. We grow by re-digesting and reworking our experiences throughout our life, and so in a sense we're never totally finished with the past. But we can certainly work through each re-emergence of old stuff. Even traumatic experiences can be healed, no matter how severe, as we climb the spiral of intimacy and emotional well being.

SEXUAL EXPRESSIONS OF CARING

Sex in early adulthood is different from what it is after forty. In mid-life, priorities shift. If we're still lusting and longing for (or engaging in) many sexual encounters, we can suspect there's some other game afoot than just not having found the right person. We may be looking for closeness but don't know how to get it except through sexuality. We may still be trying to free ourselves from constrictive sexual taboos. Or perhaps we're satisfying ourselves with the consolation prize of power through sexual conquest or the short-lived thrill of the new. Some of us may use sex to reassure ourselves we're desirable or adequate as human beings. All these reasons may underlie sexual excitement, but as we get older our deeper need for genuine closeness begins to take precedence. Now we're more likely to seek refuge with one other person, to renew ourselves and share the subtler joys of companionship. As singer Michael Franks put it, we're "getting tired of this no deposit, no return love."

It's hard to give up the old strategies and compulsive sexual behaviors when we believe everyone else is still doing it the way it was done during the days of "free love"; and even now in certain large cities casual sex is quite the thing. While the sex might be hot, and pleasure is a good thing, the point is, sexual attraction is not necessarily a good criteria for mate selection. For most people over forty, the tide has turned somewhat, as a natural part of growing older. But it's a safe bet that the person we're reaching out to has as much desire for authenticity as we do, and that the more we're ourselves, the more they will be also and the more interesting and sexy we'll be to each other. Sex is now part of an overall loving context of experience between two unique individuals.

Authenticity means being transparent, not strategizing or playing coy games. A gay friend of ours, newly in love, mentioned he had to restrain himself from revealing how eager he was to spend time with his new boyfriend, lest he seem too forward. We asked him what was the point in not doing what he felt like doing. If his new love thinks he's too forward, then it's something to explore together rather than hide. The truth needs to be told if we want genuine intimacy.

Our friend called that night to say we'd given him something to think about. He'd realized that if he had to pretend he wasn't excited and eager to spend time with his new love, he'd be tying himself in knots. What was the fun in that?

"Besides," he said, "I want him to know how I feel about him."

"If your boyfriend doesn't appreciate your excitement or doesn't reciprocate," I said, "wouldn't you rather find out early in the relationship than after you get more involved?"

Our friend made the phone call and was delighted to find his interest was returned. It was a relief to both of them to discover they each valued truthfulness. Our friend had always been candid about big issues with moral import, such as telling potential partners he was HIV positive. Ironically, it was the little things, like revealing his affection, that made him anxious.

Once a relationship has gotten onto some kind of regular footing, the initial excitement may wear off. If this happens, it's important to look for reasons why, because there are always reasons and solutions. Blockage to sexual excitement (once we've ruled out physiological problems) is usually caused by withholding fears, questions or resentments. The tiniest failure in communication will quickly show up in bed. Like the pea under the mattress in the fable of the Princess and the Pea, the tiny piece of withheld resentment or fear can be enough of an emotional irritant to inhibit sexual excitement. What doesn't get talked about before bedtime will clamor silently for expression after we've said goodnight or even in the midst of lovemaking.

Sometimes sexuality diminishes temporarily *because* we've made an intimate connection, and because we're communicating and doing everything right. Thereby we've created the trust and emotional safety in the relationship for old issues to surface, and it's the old issues reappearing that temporarily inhibit sexual attraction. They appear in order to be healed, and healing takes precedence over sexual feelings. What this means is that if we're in the midst of reliving an old experience, our energy will go to that, temporarily leaving little energy for sexuality.

When this happens, we need to maintain the perspective that this is the relationship we've longed for and created. And part of the function of relationships is to heal old wounds so we can live fully in the present. Barring other issues, once our healing is completed, our sexual energy comes back, even more intensely, because nothing from the past remains to block it.

Women are sometimes brought up to think they have to have sex even when they don't want it just to keep their partners happy. As we mature, it's harder to falsify ourselves in order to give a good sexual performance. But to be freed of the cultural imperative to perform only for the other person, we need to find out if our partner wants to exploit us or if he or she is really interested in loving us reciprocally in a sexual way. When we don't consciously understand or don't know how to articulate these dynamics, we'll work them out unconsciously. One way for women especially to do this is to lose their sexual desire, in order to see how their partners will react. If the partner doesn't force himself on her or act hurt that she doesn't want him, she'll feel reassured that he won't exploit her.

This is a common kind of testing that occurs in intimacy, and it may go on for a few months, depending on how deeply ingrained our old conditioning is. [See further discussion of testing in Chapter 4.]

Some men are brought up to think their virility is measured by how many women they conquer sexually. Such a man may unconsciously test to see if his partner needs him to be this way, or if she'll love other aspects of his personality, like how sensitive or considerate he is, or that he's not driven to have sex purely because of testosterone. In our experience, a woman who treats a man as a sensitive whole human being is more likely to evoke a sensitive response from him.

ENDINGS

If we do have to find a new partner, we don't really start over again at the beginning. We just pick up where we left off. That is to say, whatever we learned from the previous relationship is directly applied to the next. Interestingly enough, when we move on to a new relationship, we'll be drawn to a person who embodies all we still need which the previous relationship didn't fulfill. It will be differently packaged, and there will be new things as well. But we are never without opportunities to receive something we still need. That's because our unconscious mind is a brilliant ally for our growth. Any conscious wisdom we've gained from our previous relationship is supplemented by the intelligence of our unconscious mind, and wittingly or unwittingly, we draw into our lives what we're ready for next.

This is easier to observe in retrospect. When we end a relationship we're necessarily caught up in feelings of loss. This is a normal and necessary part of grieving. It's important to be with these feelings and not avoid them.

Unresolved issues or unmourned loss can show up in our next relationship and contaminate it. For that reason we suggest caution in entering a new relationship too quickly. A rebound relationship may be the perfect way to avoid pain, but it only delays the grieving process.

Statistics demand that we conclude this chapter with some thoughts on change and loss. Although 81% of college graduates in the 1980's who married after age 26 were still married 20 years later,[31] the chances remain very high that between 40 and 50 percent of first marriages started in recent years will end in either divorce or separation before one partner dies.[32] So even if we want our after-forty marriage to be the last one, it may not be, and that's not necessarily a tragedy. One of my most influential teachers met the love of his life when he was sixty-two. She became his third wife. And neither would have been ready for the other any earlier. They're magnificent together.

Commitment comes in different ways. For some, it may be simply an absence of negatives that leads to "I do," while for others it's a process of joyful and thoughtful consideration and working through whatever reservations might exist. In any case, once we commit we agree to live *as though* we'll be together for the rest of our lives.

Thoughts of what may happen down the road are usually far, far away. But fate may intervene in the most stable and happy of relationships. We suggest being open and willing at most any time to discuss unexpected endings if something were to happen, like a life-threatening illness or a catastrophic accident. "Of course," you might say, "we talk about everything. We'd certainly talk about that." But what if "that" is a roving eye, a seven-year itch, or an embarrassing mid-life crisis that could tear the relationship apart? None of that is easy to talk about. Time and again we have seen relationship-threatening infatuations arise from a reappearance of the past deeply-seated fears and anxieties we discussed in Chapter 2, commonly masquerading as "we're no longer right for each other." But what if the partners, after years of perfect compatibility, genuinely find themselves growing in ways that take them in such different directions they feel it's impossible to continue being together? And strange as it may seem, we've also known couples with one person terminally ill, who hadn't been able to talk openly about death or even to say goodbye, for fear that their partner couldn't handle it. In some cases, they never got the chance. With all the uncertainties and mind-reading that goes on when trouble knocks, how would we know much of anything without the willingness to discuss and explore our difficult and painful feelings openly and honestly? Although sometimes there really is genuine incompatibility, how would we know without the willingness to discuss and explore such difficult and painful feelings openly and honestly?

If, for example, your partner expresses a desire to leave and you say to him, "You said you'd never leave me," your anxiety may derail the real question, "Why do you feel that way?" This fantasy of leaving may only be his way of thinking about a problem that's arisen between the two of you. Since he doesn't know how to talk about the problem, or perhaps believes there's no solution, he tries to resolve it by having a fantasy about leaving. But if you could talk it through, you'd likely sort it out.

If, down the road, you both find you've completed what you came together to do, so be it. Take the next step. But be sure all the possibilities have been explored, no stone left unturned. Where to go next becomes apparent as soon as the old is completed. And our next relationship will benefit from all the accumulated wisdom of the last.

ENDING IS A PROCESS

For one person in a couple to single-handedly walk a path of authenticity is difficult. The non-participating partner may be left behind. But it's better to find out now if your partner isn't willing to walk this path with you. If that's the case, you've arrived at major crossroads.

As long as you're aware of the issues and keep them open for discussion, any decision you make will be for the best. Every problem has many levels of solution. Even if there appears to be a major rift of values, leaving may not be the best solution right now. Other work may still need to be done. So you continue working on it until the next step becomes clear. This is an ongoing process that respects each person's limits and readiness. Authenticity, including willingness and openness, is required. Authenticity is the thread that leads us out of the maze of artifice and into genuine intimacy.

4. The Path of Authenticity

"The basic reason to pursue authenticity ... is that there is nothing more important to do in this life than becoming yourself."

~ Geoff Bellman, *The Consultant's Calling*[33]

WHAT IS INTIMACY?

Intimacy has been defined many ways. Sociologist Erik Erikson[34] speaks of it as the ability to be committed to someone else and to become strong enough ethically, to keep that commitment, no matter what.

Psychologist Nathaniel Branden calls intimacy the "sharing of the self on the deepest and most personal, private level,"[35] and renowned sex researchers Masters and Johnson call it "an exchange of vulnerabilities."[36] Summing up the thoughts and reflections of many writers is the definition by Ken Keyes, Jr., that intimacy means being in touch with our emotions; communicating thoughts, feelings and desires and listening to those of our partner; genuinely appreciating and loving ourselves; deeply loving and caring for our partner; and committing ourselves to making our relationships work.[37]

The definition closest to our vision is that of Harriet Lerner. She says,

> ...intimacy means we can be who we are in a relationship and allow the other person to do the same ... An intimate relationship is one in which neither party silences, sacrifices or betrays the self, and each party displays strength and vulnerability, weakness and competence, in a balanced way.[38]

To these definitions we would add one crucial ingredient: safety. An intimate relationship has to be physically and emotionally safe enough that both partners can willingly explore whatever comes up. This safety gives us the freedom to let unconscious sources of anxiety surface so they can be understood and dealt with.

FITTING THE LOCK

How do we find someone to share intimacy with? Many of us begin our search in the wrong place, much like the person in front of his house one night under a bright street lamp, searching the ground for his keys. When a passerby offered help, he politely refused, saying, "I lost them in the house, but the light's so much better out here."

Some people are so driven by loneliness they don't look closely enough at their criteria for identifying mate material. They use standards of cultural desirability that don't necessarily have to do with compatibility. They may make long lists of likes and dislikes, preferences and opinions. They search for common ground, discuss sexual compatibility, what they like to do, politics and religion, and how many if any children they have or want. These criteria are not unimportant, but they're only introductory.

Once upon a time there was a man who wanted to find his ideal mate. He made a long list of the characteristics he wanted, then prioritized and narrowed them down to just four: physical beauty, well-rounded education, good communication skills and compatible spiritual beliefs. The first category, physical beauty, wasn't easy to satisfy, since he had a particular vision of what that meant. Once he found someone who fit his image of who he was supposed to be with, she then had to fulfill the other three conditions. His search was long and frustrating, but finally he found the perfect mate. She was everything he had dreamed of.

His friends were overjoyed, but their excitement turned to dismay when, after a few weeks, the relationship fizzled.

"What happened?" they asked. "How could it be? How could you let her slip away?"

The jilted lover turned to them and said, "I searched long and hard for her and thought I'd finally found the perfect wife. But alas, she was searching for the perfect husband."

The search for the ideal mate can be ever elusive, which is why we're advocating a different approach, an approach from the inside out. The way to find the person who fits with us is to make sure we fit with ourselves first. If we can align our inner and outer self, our public and private face, so to speak, then we will be, and be perceived as, who we really are. Not only will we be able to express what we really think, feel and want, we'll be able to do it without making others feel defensive. This clean, clear expression of an integrated, coherent personality is not only the essence of good communication, but also the basis for genuine intimacy.

IT'S NOT SO MUCH FINDING THE RIGHT PERSON AS BECOMING THE RIGHT PERSON

Lasting intimacy is possible when we're able to be fully ourselves and able to share ourselves completely with another person. This requires, above all, skill in the art of communication. Good communication is complete communication. It's the vehicle for being real with another person.

Full presence is required for this approach to work, however. Holding back defeats the process. If we can be fully ourselves and share what's on our mind and in our heart, we stay on the path.

Some people say, "I let them know everything about me and they didn't want me. So being authentic doesn't work." This is actually an illustration of how authenticity does work. This statement describes the selection process. Would you want to be with someone who didn't appreciate who you are? I remember many years ago, writing what I thought was a unique response to someone's personal ad, full of honest self-disclosure. I sent it off with high hopes, and what I thought was a complimentary, good-natured photo. A few days later I eagerly opened the reply and found my picture returned, with a note written on the back... "good luck."

If you're rejected after coming from an honest, open hearted place, it's a safe assumption that person's not "the one."

Admittedly, you may have to get through a lot of lunches while dating, but you know you're close to finding "the one" when you experience someone who does want to be with you as you really are, and vice versa. Being authentic gets you there much sooner than employing calculated strategies or trying fit the bill no matter what.

Complete communication is the essence of being authentic, but let's not abandon common sense. It's fine in a Twelve-Step meeting to introduce yourself as, say, an alcoholic, but we wouldn't recommend it on a first date. However, once you've got some mutual chemistry with someone, then it's important to disclose deeper aspects of yourself, down to the microscopic truth, and including your hopes and dreams.

One couple we worked with seldom verbalized their needs to each other. They believed love meant knowing what each other thought or wanted without having to be told. This led to various problems. For instance, the woman expected her partner to know she wanted sex when she put her arms around him. He assumed she was buttering him up for some favor she was preparing to ask him. He didn't want to leave himself open to hear her request, so he ignored her signal. Her idea was, "If you don't know, you don't love me."

She hardly ever got the sexual attention she wanted because she couldn't ask for it directly, and on it went. So much resentment built up they stopped talking to each other about things that mattered. Finally they stopped talking altogether. They still loved each other, but communication had completely broken down.

The belief that we should be mind-readers for each other stems from early childhood. It's one of those delicious fantasies we hate to give up. The problem is, while a child's needs are fairly easy to divine, adults' needs are not. We can't guess all the meanings that underlie a look, gesture, mood or action. Having to continually guess what our partner thinks and feels can generate enough anxiety to sink a ship.

Becoming an ideal mate is more the issue than finding one. That's because what we project outwardly we attract back to us. Therefore, relationships that last are those where each person continuously cultivates intimacy with the other by being as fully present for the other as possible. We call this the path of authenticity.

Although things are changing now, our culture traditionally erects barricades against self-disclosure and vulnerability. Nonetheless, many of us are unwilling to tolerate the stress that not being real creates. Get real, and you'll attract people who appreciate who you are and what you have to offer, people who are willing to be (or willing to learn how to be) real with you in return.

SEVEN STEPS TO CREATING INTIMACY

Creating genuine intimacy through authenticity is a seven-step process. The process starts with getting in touch with our feelings and then not distracting ourselves, no matter how uncomfortable it may be. This includes staying conscious from moment to moment to avoid slipping into old patterns. The seven steps are as follows:

1. Allowing and skillfully processing feelings.

2. Communicating so others really hear you.

3. Listening non-defensively and understanding the power of silence.

4. Staying present (Mindfulness).

5. Taking emotional risks.

6. Letting go.

7. Self-forgiveness.

Although most of us intuitively believe in these steps, few of us have had much practice or support for actually following and living them. These behaviors feel emotionally risky. We'll show you how to take the emotional risks which keep relationships fresh and exciting. We'll also show how the ten beliefs that destroy intimacy, discussed in Chapter 2, tie in with each step and can sabotage our best intention and effort to follow them.

These steps are most effective if done in the context of an intimate relationship. This is because intimacy brings up issues which usually don't arise otherwise. But in case you're not currently in an intimate relationship and decide to use these seven steps, they'll have both subtle and obvious effects on you. We predict that not long after starting this process – if you really want it and are internally ready – you will meet someone with whom you can share intimacy, or significantly deepen an on-going relationship.

STEP 1. ALLOWING AND SKILLFULLY PROCESSING FEELINGS

Long-standing traditions tell us that we are, by virtue of being human, entitled to our full measure, including all our feelings. Buddhist teacher Pema Chödrön says "It's very helpful to realize that the emotions we have, the negativity and the positivity, are exactly what we need to be fully human, fully awake, fully alive."[39] Paying attention to our feelings, naming them, and learning how to skillfully process them without wounding ourselves or harming innocent bystanders, may be unfamiliar activities. Most of us grew up feeling lots of things we had no names for. We had no name for the pain we felt or for the pain our parents felt but didn't dare admit.

Although many of our readers are not "Boomers," the Baby Boom generation (1946-1964), our generation, had a particularly hard time with emotional vulnerability.

We grew up in relatively stable surroundings. We had a stable middle class with economic security (in my family, both my parents worked). Schools were funded adequately; we had a chance to get an education. On the surface, the American dream was there for the asking and the taking.

But there was a dark side to this picture. Underneath the shiny comfortable surfaces was often a profound psychological emptiness and lack of purpose. Fascination with commodities and technology had been promoted at the expense of human connection.[40] To speak of feelings was something only women did with each other, and if they couldn't do that, they became depressed or "over-emotional" in their frustrated attempts to get their emotionally removed or authoritarian husbands to acknowledge subjective, non-rational experience.

Once the children started to grow up, husbands and wives turned to each other, often to find they didn't know who the other was anymore, if they ever did. And they didn't have ways to relate to each other outside traditional roles.

Rarely prepared to enter the work-force, mothers often turned to the solace of alcohol. (It wasn't called alcoholism in those days unless one was falling-down drunk.) Or they clung to their children and smothered them with incessant yet perfunctory attentions. Fathers, who had been trained to fight wars and bring home the paycheck, had never learned to talk about their feelings. They held their emotions back from view and refused to share problems or feelings of confusion or pain (absolutely necessary on the battlefield but not very functional at home). Many men turned to alcohol to deal with war trauma or to mask feelings of other kinds.

Our parents' attitudes toward war were symptomatic of how far alienation had progressed. Their generation carried the scientific rationale so far as to consider thinking the unthinkable – accepting nuclear war as a reasonable option. Elementary schools participated in the delusion by teaching us to protect ourselves in case of nuclear attack by crawling under our desks. How much further can emotional denial go? So although traditional roles may have been part of the "security" we grew up with, they constrained our parents emotionally, and those lessons were passed on to us.

Growing up in these environments, we felt the pain but had no way to talk about it and no way of knowing we were not alone in having these feelings. We suspected something was wrong, but speaking of such things was "just not done." So there was little alternative but to bury the pain of trauma deep inside and avoid anything that might trigger it, including intimacy.

Since we hadn't learned to share openly what was going on inside us, we weren't able to see that the primary responsibility for our problems, and for their solutions, lay within ourselves. Instead we tended to look for someone else to blame and were therefore seldom able to make use of our early romantic relationships as vehicles for self-awareness and personal growth.

Following the baby boom came the baby bust, and over-40 Busters are no strangers to these dynamics either. In fact, there is no magical inoculation against emotional denial. Even if we as parents and grandparents become skillful "emotionalists," Gen X, Gen Y, and all generations to come will have to pay attention and practice authenticity to maintain that skill. Self-protection, even in the form of denial and at the high price of emotional isolation, is a natural human impulse and has its place. It should go without saying that we have to protect ourselves from physical and emotional danger. But once in relationship, if we are still emotionally aloof, we might well ask why. As a single person we are not beholden to anyone on a daily, intimate basis. Not so once in relationship. Our actions, self-protective or otherwise, must now somehow become more inclusive. No matter how good the role models, it seems that we still need guidelines, maps, and reminders that feelings, and the willingness to risk communicating about them, are what connect us – and keep us connected – to each other. Being compliant or "nice," or playing roles, instead of expressing what we really think and feel prevents true connection with others and will only increase our sense of loneliness.

But we need the right words to accurately express what we feel. Most of us, educated as we may be, have only a limited "feeling" vocabulary. We have difficulty identifying our emotions and may therefore ignore them until they turn into physical sensations, so intense that we feel out of control, overwhelmed, or our feelings erupt inappropriately. The amount of upset, anxiety, or fear that an outburst of temper can cause doesn't lessen after forty.

We may not suspect a connection between physical sensation and feelings, but the somatization of feelings is so common that an estimated 75% of medical problems brought to the attention of general medical practitioners are classified as stress-related.[41] The symptoms range from asthma to ulcers, and include tight muscles, stomach aches, high blood pressure, migraines, insomnia, chronic fatigue, lower back pain, constipation and indigestion, to name a few. Some experts have even described a connection between stress and viral disease, cancer and auto-immune disorders.

Many of us have difficulty identifying our emotions and may therefore ignore them until they turn into physical sensations.

We know a couple who can stay together only if they are both ill. The man had a childhood so full of emotional neglect he never was able to ask for what he wanted emotionally. As an adult, he could indulge himself in buying expensive grown-up toys, but he could only feel entitled to being emotionally looked after if he was sick.

He developed a mysterious illness no doctor could cure, which ensured him long-term medical attention and caretaking from his wife. Ironically, she was only able to stop shouldering the burden for both of them by developing an equally serious illness, which forced her to take a break and relax now and then.

* * *

Some people try to edit their feelings – to express the pleasant ones and hold back difficult ones. But it's not possible to limit certain feelings and retain full access to others. For example, turning down the volume on anger, the most difficult emotion for many of us, turns down the volume on all the rest. The most common result of repressed anger is depression. The reason is that by repressing awareness of this powerful emotion, all our emotions are dampened and our vitality along with them.

We have thousands of feelings every day, and it would be impractical to be aware of every little emotional change we go through. But we should have the ability to put our finger on whatever we're feeling at any given time. We also need to share our emotional experience to validate and confirm our perceptions and emotional responses (bubbles and social vacuums have serious repercussions).

Language reflects our need for and attempts at mastery. For example, people living in very cold climates, reliant on snow and ice, develop many words with precise meanings because of the survival value of knowing these things. English is rich in emotional expression, but apart from English majors and other voracious readers, most of us are fine with "mad," "bad," "sad," and "glad." To help fill this void, we've provided a Feeling Vocabulary chart on the following pages with many gradations of feelings. We invite you to use it to explore your own world of feelings. As with cultivating any new habit, paying regular attention to our inner experience may feel awkward at first, but you may be pleasantly surprised at what you discover after a day or two.

Make a few copies of the chart, which you may need for the exercises that follow. A good start in using the chart on a daily basis is to check in with yourself every hour for a few days by asking, "What am I feeling right now?" Use the chart for accuracy and keep track of all this in a binder, notebook or daily planner. Then proceed to the exercises at the end of this chapter.

There are also some exercises coming up in Step Two for increasing familiarity with our own emotional world. As with cultivating any new habit, paying regular attention to our inner experience may feel awkward at first, but you may be pleasantly surprised at what you discover after a day or two.

FEELING VOCABULARY CHART

MIRTH	PLEASURE	DISTRESS
AMUSED	AMIABLE	PERPLEXED
CHEERFUL	CALM	FRETFUL
DELIGHTED	EASY	MOODY
JOVIAL	WARM	IMPATIENT
CONVIVIAL	PLEASED	UNCOMFORT-
CAREFREE	HAPPY	ABLE
GAY	PEACEFUL	FRUSTRATED
GLEEFUL	TOUCHED	GUILTY
JOLLY	PLEASED	OVERWHELMED
LIGHTHEARTED	RELAXED	DISTRACTED
MERRY	RELIEVED	TRAPPED
ELATED	SATISFIED	DISSONANT
ENTHUSED	SERENE	DISCONTENT
EXCITED	TENDER	DISPLEASED
JOYOUS	COMFORTED	DISSATISFIED
JUBILANT	CONTENTED	DISTURBED
EXUBERANT	EXCITED	REGRETFUL
THRILLED	AMOROUS	HURT
ECSTATIC	ENTHRALLED	ANGUISHED
EXAULTED	BLISSFUL	PAINED
		PERTURBED

ANGER	*GRIEF*	*FEAR*
ANNOYED	BLUE	CONCERNED
IMPATIENT	SAD	EDGY
IRRITATED	DISAPPOINTED	UNCERTAIN
PUT OUT	DISCOURAGED	INSECURE
DISMAYED	GLOOMY	GUARDED
UPTIGHT	LONELY	APPREHENSIVE
PERTURBED	LOST	ANXIOUS
RESENTFUL	GLUM	NERVOUS
FRUSTRATED	MELANCHOLY	SHY
AGGRAVATED	LEFT OUT	GUILTY
CRITICAL	SORROWFUL	WORRIED
RANKLED	UNHAPPY	LEERY
RILED	DISMAL	EMBARRASSED
DISGUSTED	DEJECTED	DEFENSIVE
MAD	DEFLATED	AFRAID
FED UP	DEPRESSED	FRIGHTENED
ANGRY	DESPAIRINNG	IMTIMIDATED
ENRAGED	HOPELESS	TERRIFIED

DISGUST	*RESOLUTION*	*WONDER*
AVERSION	ASSURED	INTERESTED
REPELLED	CERTAIN	CURIOUS
REPULSED	SURE	INTRIGUED
ASHAMED	PERSUASIVE	BEMUSED
INADEQUATE	GRATEFUL	PUZZLED
DISDAIN	DEVOTED	PERPLEXED
CONTEMPT	CONFIDENT	BAFFLED
REVOLTED	DETERMINED	CONFUSED
APPALLED	ENCOURAGED	SURPRISED
AGHAST	PROUD	ENCHANTED
ABHORRED	HARDY	BEWILDERED
HUMILIATED	STRONG	AMAZED
LOATHING	FIRM	ASTONISHED
NAUSEATED	ASSERTIVE	STARTLED
SCORNFUL	POTENT	AWED
SICKENED	RESOLVED	ASTOUNDED

EXERCISES FOR IDENTIFYING FEELINGS

1. Circle the feelings in the preceding feeling table which you have most often and which you believe characterize you most accurately. Note down (we recommend dedicating a notebook for these exercises) those which are difficult for you to share with others and why.

    a. How do you handle these feelings when they come up?

    b. Who are the people in your life (present and past) who discouraged you from having your feelings in general?

c. Which feelings in particular did they discourage?

d. What can you imagine their reasons were?

e. Who were the people in your life (past and present) who encouraged and supported you having all your feelings?

g. What do you think their motives were?

h. In what ways are you supportive of others having their feelings?

i. Do you allow yourself the same emotional freedom?

2. Note each of the feelings on the chart that – when you encounter them in others – make you even the least bit uncomfortable.

a. For each feeling you've noted, try to describe the discomfort and why you think it makes you uncomfortable.

b. Although having all sorts of feelings is commonplace, why wouldn't you want to be a person who *regularly* gets in that mood?

c. What is the most recent example you can think of when you acted or felt that way?

d. What triggered the feeling?

e. How did you deal with it?

Not every feeling, or mood, is uncomfortable or upsetting. For example, anger, one of the more difficult feelings to deal with, can come and go like a summer storm and simply clear the air. But some people cannot tolerate even that.

Why are feelings that make us most uncomfortable important? You may find the attributes or characteristics we dislike most or find most disquieting in others are those we dislike in ourselves.

Aversion to, or even criticism of, these shadow parts of ourselves is a way of distancing ourselves from them. There is a price to be paid for ignoring our dark side.

Having a dark side, or 'shadow,' is not the issue, because we all have our less than noble parts. It's that they are not sealed off, locked out of awareness. When we're tired or stressed they can grab us unawares and we "lose it." It's an authentic response, but we're out of control. It's far better to drop the illusion of a flawless character and learn how to co-exist and skillfully deal with our demons. We advocate coming to terms with who we are, all of it.

THE PROBLEM OF ANGER

Anger is the most misunderstood emotion. When misused or repressed, it can do great harm, yet when understood and used appropriately, it can be one of our greatest allies. The inability to deal with anger has been cited as one of the top three reasons for the early break-up of marriages.[42] Anger is not a mysterious force that comes and goes. Like love, anger has a cause, meaning and intention. According to Harriet Lerner, anger is an important signal, often warning us that we may be trying to choose "between having a relationship and having a self."[43]

(Anger) may be a signal that we're being hurt, that our rights are being violated, that our needs or wants are not being adequately met, or simply that something isn't right. Our anger may tell us that we're not addressing an important emotional issue in our lives. Our anger may be a signal that we're doing more and giving more than we can comfortably do or give. Or our anger may warn us that others are doing too much for us, at the expense of our own competence and growth.[44]

Anger can be self-affirming in important ways:

> Just as physical pain tells us to take our hand off the hot stove, the pain of our anger preserves the very integrity of our self. Our anger can motivate us to say 'no' to the ways in which we're defined by others and 'yes' to the dictates of our inner self.[45]

As Dr. Lerner points out, anger is a secondary, not a primary, emotion. It's a signal that something else, which preceded it and is going on underneath it, needs attention.

For example, two young women were accompanying some pre-schoolers on an outing. Suddenly one of the children darted into the street chasing a ball. One woman grabbed the startled child and yanked him back onto the sidewalk, shouting at him angrily as the child began to cry.

All this happened very quickly. First the woman felt heart-stopping fear. Then, in response to the fear, and perhaps to deflect it, she yelled at the child. By getting angry, she could quell her fear. The anger also covered the guilt she felt for not having watched closely enough.

If the woman stayed in touch with these primary emotions, uncomfortable as it might have been to face them, she'd not only be in touch with what was most real for her at that moment but would also be able to give the child accurate feedback instead of a "you're bad" message. She could say to the child, "I was terrified you'd be hit by a car!" And then, "I feel angry that you ran out into the street."

As mentioned earlier, anger is difficult for so many of us because of our background and conditioning. Rare were the parents who expressed anger directly and appropriately. More commonly, they either stockpiled their anger and frustrations until they exploded in fits of fury, expressed it indirectly in manipulative or cutting ways, or repressed it and got depressed as a result. This modeling left its mark on us.

For example, if we grew up with a parent who had an explosive temper, we might want to avoid anger at all costs. As one client said of his father:

I never knew when he would blow up. I'd say something and *Wham!* He'd be on me out of nowhere ... I knew what I had said, but it [his father's anger] didn't make sense. It was out of proportion and inappropriate, but as a child I didn't know that. For me, that was what being angry was all about, and I wanted no part of it.

This client was neither timid nor shy, yet became alarmed when any adult male showed the slightest sign of disapproval. This made it very difficult for him to work for a male boss. Although he liked the environment and benefits of a corporate job, he had been self-employed for years.

Others in a similar situation might identify with the angry parent and later in life become abusive in disagreements with their partners, wounding with sarcasm, accusations or blame.

Or, someone who grew up in a home where anger was not tolerated might logically conclude that anger was bad, that nothing can be changed by being angry, or that no one has a right to feel angry in the first place. Such people may cut themselves off from awareness of their own anger, or invalidate it.

If our well of rage is so deep that we believe getting in touch with it will prove dangerous or even lethal for ourselves or another, then we may employ all available means not to feel it, from rigid denial to anesthetizing ourselves with drugs, alcohol, food or nicotine. Seeing a counselor or psychotherapist is a good way to work through this issue. In the safety of the counseling/psychotherapy relationship, we can learn how to raise our awareness of anger as it develops, and experience it a little at a time so as not to be overwhelmed. We can also learn how to express anger in appropriate, non-destructive ways.

After understanding that we can control our anger, we then need to recognize it when it arises. Although most men have little trouble with this, women are subject to strong cultural restraints. As Dr. Lerner points out,

> The taboos against (women) feeling and expressing anger are so powerful that even *knowing* when we are angry is not a simple matter. When a woman shows her anger, she's likely to be dismissed as irrational or worse.... Because the very possibility that we're angry often meets with rejection and disapproval from others, it's no wonder that it's hard for us to know, let alone admit, that we're angry.[44]

Although anger is the "fallback emotion" for most guys, many men are also burdened in this way if they were raised in households where similar values prevailed. However, whenever it appears, once we're aware of it, we need to look for its source and be sure we're dealing with the right issue. It's amazing how frequently we march off to battle without knowing what the war is all about. We may be putting our anger energy into trying to change or control a person who doesn't want to change, rather than putting that same energy into getting clear about our own needs and choices. This is especially true in our closest relationships, where, if we don't learn to use our anger first to clarify our own thoughts, feelings, priorities and choices, we can easily get trapped in endless cycles of fighting and blaming.[45]

Sometimes the anger one or both of us feel may have little or nothing to do with each other. Instead we may be experiencing old anger from early trauma, triggered by something in the present, but whose fires are fanned by the past. As one client put it, "We are steeped in our childhood experiences like a house filled with smoke."

I may think I'm angry at my partner when, in fact, he's merely done something which reminds me of a past experience I'm still angry about. There's nothing wrong in having the feeling – or any feeling, for that matter. In fact, it's essential, but we need to recognize that in this case our partner is only a reminder. The identifying mark of old anger is its inappropriate intensity

Outside of counseling/psychotherapy, the best way to protect our relationships from old anger is to be on the look-out for it and explore it when it pops up (which it will). Unless identified, old anger has emotional charge and destructive impact, because we'll project it onto our current relationship. It leaks out in indirect ways.

Anger displacement – when we "leak" it out inappropriately onto the wrong target – can show up in our self-talk. It can take the form of judgments, accusations or even the curses we silently hurl at passing strangers, other drivers, people in the supermarket. It can show up in cruel little thoughts we may have about others, especially those we are closest to. It's important to talk about these thoughts if they are impacting a significant relationship. Then we can get to the real issue underneath. Our self-talk is often a bridge to unconscious feelings which are just coming to our attention.

Another clue that we may be sitting on old anger is when we create distance just as we begin to feel close to our partner. We may start a fight over something small if we feel too close, creating a safe distance and erecting a barrier around our repressed anger. Or we may suddenly feel critical or contemptuous of our partner, when just a short time ago he or she seemed perfectly reasonable and acceptable.

By sharing our negative thoughts matter of factly, *as information about ourselves rather than as judgments or criticisms,* we become aware of our deeper feelings. And as we get into the habit of self-disclosure, we get more comfortable with it. If our partner is also trying to walk the path of authenticity, this process is not fraught with danger or destructive in any way. It is a pressure relief valve bringing release with awareness. Mutual self-disclosure, what we call "keeping current," increases intimacy.

MOODS

Lots of people, especially women, experience "moods," and both sexes tend to write them off, or excuse them, like "It's just that time of month," or "I'm just in a mood," as though it were a virus that mysteriously appears and disappears. Moods, however, are actually the unidentified emotional component of some unresolved experience. A mood can be a symptom of old anger, from the recent or distant past, of depression, of fear/anxiety, of loneliness, etc.

One person expressed it this way:

> Speaking from personal experience, before I got into psychotherapy, I had a lot of "moods" which were most troubling and seemingly unavoidable and inescapable. Once I learned how to see them as a signal of some deeper issue and learned how to decode them, I could work through the issues and gradually the moods became less frequent.
>
> Now, if I do get into a mood, I pay attention to it. I look closer to identify what event triggered it, then I dig deeper to find what it is I'm really disturbed about. Once I understand what that is, I can stop being upset and decide what to do about it.

Conscious awareness is at least part of the key to handling our moods. Moods are like a vague fog of feeling, but feelings don't appear out of thin air. They are triggered by thoughts or memories, and negative thoughts trigger negative emotions. Negative thoughts are powerful because they contain a kernel of truth, but they are only half-truths. One powerful way to get out of a mood is to gain a conscious, fuller and more accurate perspective by sleuthing out the thought associated with the mood, then following that thread back to uncover the missing evidence disconfirming the negative thought. A new, balanced perspective dramatically changes the picture and can lift us out of a serious downer.

We would like to recommend an excellent workbook to guide you through this particular process: *Mind Over Mood*, by Greenberger and Padesky.[47]

VICTIM ANGER

If we feel victimized, rightly or wrongly, our anger may be expressed destructively. We may lash out indiscriminately and desperately if we believe our survival is at stake. We may experience feelings of helplessness, revenge and retaliation and express our anger through these filters. Victim anger is what starts vendettas and feuds.

These intense feelings are often fully justified and seldom managed well. The following remarks pertain to situations that are not life-threatening, where choices can be made without physical or emotional harm.

Taking a victim, or "one-down" position prevents the balanced sharing of power and feelings that intimacy demands. We can fall into the victim trap in a number of ways: if we let our rights be violated, submit to unfair circumstances, act helpless and out of control, fail to acknowledge our own contribution to our problems, sacrifice our growth to bolster or protect someone else, stay in a bad relationship, or feel guilty if we get angry when it's appropriate to feel that way.

Victim anger is only resolved when we take responsibility for our part in whatever circumstances are causing the imbalance and the pain. Because it is unfocused, victim anger provokes defensiveness in the other person, because usually the victim doesn't say what s/he wants. Instead, s/he blames or accuses the other, who is helpless to do anything because s/he doesn't know what *to* do.

Rather than inflict our bad moods or undeserved anger on our partner, we need to take responsibility for it. We can decode our moods, talk about rather than act out anger or other feelings of upset, and thoroughly explore where the upset or anger comes from. Often we'll discover that old issues are involved. Once identified, we can see what changes are possible and determine if we're willing to make them.

WE CAN CHOOSE TO FEEL ENTITLED

This kind of victim anger can be resolved by a shift in our attitude toward ourselves. We needn't agree to be victims. We have a choice. We can feel *entitled* to good treatment and we can insist on getting it.

However, there may be impediments from within working to derail these efforts.

In Chapter 2 we cited ten beliefs that can destroy intimacy. The tenth one is perhaps the most pernicious of the lot – the belief that we are damaged goods, unworthy and out of reach of life's bounty. This belief directly interferes with standing up for ourselves as we realign the emotional forces in our lives. We've all heard variations on these terrible messages, and they don't always come from someone else! Some examples:

"You'll never be the best...there will always be someone better than you..."

"You'd forget your head if it weren't screwed on..."

"You can't cut the mustard."

"I keep comparing myself to my old self, and I don't measure up."

"I don't deserve good things."

You'll notice the "ghost parent" speaking in some of these examples. But if you think about it, you may often find that you've internalized that harsh, critical voice and taken over the job of putting yourself down.

Anger is different if it's backed up by a feeling of legitimate entitlement – knowing we deserve good treatment. This is what we call appropriate anger, and it has a liberating energy. This kind of anger is empowering. When using the energy of our anger appropriately, we can speak from strength about what's wrong and say clearly what we want or need. Appropriate anger communicates, "It's not okay to treat me this way. What I want instead is ... [you get to fill in the blank]."

Appropriate anger doesn't blame, accuse, judge, criticize, control, manipulate, withhold or physically abuse. It's direct and clean, and it's finished as soon as it's fully expressed and understood by the person we're angry with. Appropriate anger doesn't bear a grudge.

If our anger is toward someone who's no longer available to hear it, such as an absent or deceased parent, another figure from the past, or someone who's simply too closed or defensive to hear it, it's enough just to acknowledge to ourselves that we're angry, feel entitled to good treatment, and then let go of it. Letting go is different from dissociating or denying our anger; it's giving it over after it's been fully acknowledged. We'll discuss letting go further in Step 6.

Anger is indeed a two-edged sword. But in our experience working with many individuals and couples, if the flow of feeling is free and clear (meaning that we are co-existing with our moods and skillfully handling them rather than being at their mercy), and up-to-date (meaning that we keep current with ourselves and our partner about what's going on inside of us), then anger is simply a part of the panoply of emotional expression, and not a threat.

ANGER EXERCISES

1. THE INVENTORY

Anger is a basic human emotion which plays an important role in the way we communicate with others. This inventory offers you an opportunity to make an objective self study of how anger affects you and how you deal with it in your daily contacts with others. Increased awareness on your part may provide insights and clues for feeling more comfortable with yourself as well as for improving your relationships.[48]

DIRECTIONS:

Answer each question as quickly as you can, according to the way you feel right now (not the way you usually feel or felt last week).

Don't consult with anyone while completing the inventory. You may discuss it with someone after you've completed it. The value of this exercise will be lost if you change any answer during or after the discussion. Honesty is necessary.

Use the following examples for practice. Answer each question with "yes," "no," or "sometimes," to show how the question applies to your situation.

Read each question carefully. If you can't give the exact answer to a question, answer the best you can, but be sure to answer each one. There are no right or wrong answers. Answer according to the way *you* feel *at the present time.*

1. Do you admit you're angry when asked by someone else?

2. Do you have a tendency to take your anger out on someone other than the person you're angry with?

3. When you're angry with someone, do you discuss it with that person?

4. Do you keep things in until you finally explode with anger?

5. Do you pout or sulk for a long time (a couple of days or so) when someone hurts your feelings?

6. Do you disagree with others even though you feel they might get angry?

7. Are you physically abusive when you get angry?

8. Does it upset you a great deal when someone disagrees with you?

9. Do you express your ideas when they differ from those around you?

10. Do you have a tendency to be very critical of others?

11. Are you satisfied with the way you settle your differences with others?

12. Is it very difficult for you to say nice things to others?

13. Do you have good control of your temper?

14. Do you become depressed very easily?

15. When a problem arises between you and another person, do you discuss it without losing control of your emotions?

16. Do you have a tendency to put other people down (criticize)?

17. When someone has hurt your feelings, do you discuss the matter with that person?

18. Do you have frequent arguments?

19. Do you often fee/like hitting someone?

20. Is it possible for you to feel anger at someone you love?

21. Do you have a strong urge to do something harmful?

22. Do you keep your cool (control) when you're angry with someone?

23. Do you feel bad or guilty after getting angry at someone?

24. When you become angry, do you pull away or withdraw from people?

25. When someone is angry with you, do you automatically or quickly strike back with your own feelings of anger?

26. Are you aware when you're angry?

27. Provided the timing is appropriate, do you express your angry feelings without exploding?

28. Do you tend to make cutting remarks to others?

29. Do you control yourself when things don't go your way?

30. Do you feel anger is a normal emotion?

SCORING KEY FOR THE INVENTORY OF ANGER COMMUNICATION

ITEM	YES	NO	SOMETIMES
1	3	0	2
2	0	3	1
3	3	0	2
4	0	3	1
5	0	3	1
6	3	0	2
7	0	3	1
8	0	3	1
9	3	0	2
10	0	3	1
11	3	0	2
12	0	3	1
13	3	0	2
14	0	3	1
15	3	0	2
16	0	3	1
17	3	0	2
18	0	3	1
19	0	3	1
20	3	0	2
21	0	3	1
22	3	0	2
23	0	3	1
24	0	3	1
25	0	3	1
26	3	0	2
27	3	0	2
28	0	3	1
29	3	0	2
30	3	0	2

INTERPRETING YOUR SCORE

Go back to the questionnaire. In the right margin, after the column marked "Sometimes", write down your score for each item as indicated by the table above. For example, if you answered "yes" to item one, mark down a score of 3. If you answered "no" your score would be 0, and if you answered "sometimes" your score would be 2. Once you've done this for all the items, add up your total score.

The three possible responses, "yes," "no," and "sometimes," are scored from zero to three with a favorable response given the higher score. In some instances the "yes" response may be favorable, in others, unfavorable, depending on the wording of the item. The possible range of scores is from zero to ninety. The higher the sum of scores, the more effectively you are handling your angry feelings.

2. CHECK YOURSELF OUT

Write down the first thing that comes to your mind when you read the following words or phrases. Be honest with yourself in order to gain the most from this exercise.

1. When people get mad they should...

2. Feeling angry is...

3. People who get angry are...

4. When I get angry I...

5. I get angry when...

6. People make me angry when...

7. When my father got angry he...

8. When my mother got angry she...

9. The best way to describe myself is by saying...

DON'T GET LOST IN OTHERS' EXPECTATIONS

As your emotional awareness grows, your skill in recogniz-ing your own feelings increases. The next step is to extend that awareness into interactions with others. It's one thing to recognize how we feel from moment to moment when we're by ourselves. It's quite another to stay aware of what happens when we start interacting. At that point, dynamics of the old family system may become active. If we're not on top of it, these compelling vestigial forces induce us in turn to act in ways that are often dysfunctional and unnecessarily self-sacrificial. We suggest watching out partic-ularly for *identification* and *compliance*. These two mechanisms underlie many grim beliefs we may have developed early on and still carry around with us unconsciously, impacting our personal growth and interfering with our attempts to have successful rela-tionships. Jules Pfeiffer nailed these in one of his cartoons:

> "I grew up to have my father's looks, my father's speech patterns, my father's posture, my father's opinions, and my mother's contempt for my father."

Compliance and identification are unconscious, "maladaptive responses to traumatic experiences" we suffered early on. Motivated by love, loyalty, and intrinsic generosity, the child tries to protect the parent from his or her own disappointment, anger, and scorn about being mistreated. Out of compliance, the child acts as if his or her mistreatments were well deserved. If identified with the parent, the child mimics the parent who mistreated him/her.[49]

Dr. Joseph Weiss, one of the progenitors of Control Mastery Theory [see www.sfprg.org], explains compliance this way:

> Another patient I analyzed was, in childhood, frequently punished by his mother for being messy and, in particular, for failing to keep his room neat and tidy. The patient had observed that his mother, who was often depressed, seemed to enjoy punishing him. He inferred that his mother wanted him to be messy so that she could have the pleasure of punishing him. ...the patient's provocative messiness seemed at first glance to express his defiance of his mother. However, in fact, it more directly expressed a powerful wish to make her happy by complying with her.[50]

When these forces are still operative in our psyche as adults, they can cause serious disruption to our relationships. We feel drawn or compelled to act or think the way we thought our parents would have expected us to, despite feeling or knowing that it isn't in our own best interest to do so. This is illustrated by a patient of Dr. Weiss:

Mrs. A. pictured herself as having done whatever she could to rescue her mother and to make her feel loved and important...To restore her mother, Mrs. A. gave up other important activities, accomplishments, and relationships as well. She was usually not aware of making sacrifices; she would simply lose interest in relationships or accomplishments that she had valued previously...Out of guilt toward her mother, Mrs. A. gave up her first boyfriend at age 18...the first and only man she had ever loved... Mrs. A. had felt that her mother's chronic depression was growing worse as her own happiness with her boyfriend increased. After a while her mother demanded that she break off with her boyfriend because, according to her mother, he was disloyal to her. The mother's emphysema then flared up, following which the patient lost interest in her boyfriend and terminated the relationship. Unconsciously Mrs. A. believed that her mother experienced her involvement with her boyfriend as an act of disloyalty.[51]

Both require us to abandon our own experience, needs or perspective. What draws or compels us into self-abandonment may be apparent, but the actual forces are much more likely to, be subtle or even out of conscious awareness.

On the one hand, this powerful draw may be our built-in altruism expressing itself, the natural compassion human beings feel for one another from a very tender age. It is observed in infants as young as ten months.

[*Authors' note:* There is evidence in the field of developmental psychology that infants respond empathically when they perceive family members' distress, even from the age of ten months, and that by eighteen to twenty-four months they can be observed performing care-giving actions.[52]]

On the other hand, this otherwise benevolent tendency can turn into harmful self-sacrifice, as we saw in the case of Mrs. A., cited by Dr. Weiss.

* * *

A less dramatic example of how commonplace compliance is, would be what sometimes happens when we, as adults, visit our parents, who still regard us as their "kids." Suddenly, as we cross the threshold, we may feel like we're about nine years old and even start behaving differently as well, complying with their expectations.

Compliance can take many forms, such as acting out of control so someone else can feel in control; acting dumb so another can feel smart; acting inferior so another can feel superior, acting incompetent so another can feel competent; acting irresponsible so another can feel in charge; acting unsure so another can feel more sure of himself, and so on.

Compliance has been socially sanctioned for women, who for generations were counseled by their mothers and by the culture in general never to appear competent, smart or aggressive, but to act weak, vulnerable and helpless, in order to make a man feel secure and confident. After marriage another scenario emerged: "until strife do us part."

As we discussed in Chapter 2, the groundwork for self-abandonment is laid in childhood. Back then we may have abandoned ourselves psychologically in order to survive, keep the family together, protect our parents or significant others from their own weaknesses and bolster them up. But when we're adults, this behavior holds us back.

If we want relationships that foster our growth and happiness, we must refuse to give up who we are. True companionship supports us to be authentic.

Similar to compliance, but different in important ways, is identification. This is a way we may react to having a parent who is needy or insecure. We feel pressured to abandon ourselves and, in this type of situation, we respond by acting like that needy parent acts, responding in the ways they do, out of identification with him or her. The unconscious reason for our doing this is to avoid making the parent feel threatened or abandoned, as we imagine they would be by our being a separate individual in our own right, perhaps very different from them. We unconsciously imagine they need the reinforcement of our being just like them, of our reflecting themselves back to them. As children, our survival may have required us to succumb to these pressures, out of fear (sometimes justified) that a parent might reject, abandon or punish us. Often we continue to wear this "disguise," or false persona, into adulthood, since we're not aware that we're "not being ourselves."

These two processes are illustrated by the concept, now happily somewhat out of favor, of the "identified patient," or IP in a family (usually a child), as described by psychologist Virginia Satir. The IP is motivated by feelings of loyalty and guilt, to support a dysfunctional family system and protect his/her parents.

To paraphrase Satir, an IP not only takes on the parent(s) pain, but also scapegoats him/herself in order to create such a ruckus that the family is forced to get help.[53] In this way, the IP raises parental anxiety, allowing their negative expectations about, and messages to, the IP to appear as if they are true. The sacrificial lamb not only personifies the problem(s), but also is ascribed and accepts the blame for whatever problem(s) exists in the family.[54] This is all in the service of perhaps the most ubiquitous of all human endeavors: to find meaning in even the worst imaginable situations and experiences.

Any old, hidden childhood agreement to give up part of ourselves to go along with another's needs will manifest in our adult relationships until we are somehow able, consciously or unconsciously, to make the emotional decision to revoke that agreement. Identification and compliance are two of the most powerful obstacles to intimacy.

***

The story of Jim and Ellen illustrates how compliance and identification can cool a hot relationship. Jim met Ellen at a book-signing party. This was an auspicious beginning. They shared a love of good stories as well as other important things. Ellen was divorced, with a young son. Jim had never married and loved kids.

They both had careers as helping professionals and wanted to settle down. Besides that, they had great chemistry. It seemed like a match made in heaven.

Ellen knew who she was, where she wanted to go, and who she wanted to go there with. She had her preferences and opinions and didn't mince words.

Jim, on the other hand, was a "SNAG," a Sensitive, New Age Guy. He was in touch with his feelings, able to speak openly about them and be vulnerable. He was everything he thought a good partner should be: a good boy scout, he was helpful, friendly, courteous, kind, obedient, cheerful, thrifty, brave, clean, and reverent too. He always paid attention to Ellen's needs and never tried to force himself or his views on her. He thought this was what she liked in a man. When asked about dinner arrangements he always said, "whatever you'd like," or "wherever you'd like to go." Jim thought he was the ideal mate.

But Jim's father was an authoritarian type who felt he knew everything and expected obedience. To protect himself from his father's criticism and rejecting dismissals of Jim's own preferences, Jim learned to keep quiet and model his behavior after his mother, who was cheerfully respectful. He noticed that his mother often got her way, but not surprisingly for a youngster, he couldn't figure that one out.

About three months after they met, Ellen abruptly ended the relationship. It hit Jim like a ton of bricks. What went wrong? Everything had been so beautiful. When he finally caught his breath and asked Ellen exactly what had happened, she put it very simply: "Jim, you're *so* nice I don't know who you are."

Jim's interaction with someone whose approval he desperately wanted triggered compliance to the old family rules, that it was the right and expected thing to play second fiddle, complying by silence to give Ellen hegemony, and identifying with his mother's attitude but without her cleverness to work in her own agenda. Jim was trying so hard to be exactly what he thought Ellen wanted that he left out the one thing she really did want – him – his special brand of self, his quirks and preferences, all the things about him that were unique and which she had originally liked about him when she first met him, before they got involved. She didn't want homogenized milk. She didn't want a man walking on eggshells around her so as not to impose. She wanted to come up against his uniqueness with her own.

Compliance and identification are at the root of many other "transgressions" which spoil relationships. For example, promiscuous behavior (when not caused by early sexual abuse) can be based either on identification with a promiscuous parent, obedience to an unspoken rule that it would threaten the emotional connection with parents if one were to have a happier, more successful relationship than theirs, or a frustration within our own relationship because we can't be ourselves. [Note: If these ideas intrigue you, see *Imaginary Crimes: Why We Punish Ourselves and How to Stop,* by Engel and Ferguson.[55]]

A relationship can also be spoiled when one or both partners – even newlyweds – act like their parents and lose their individuality. Contrary to popular belief, this is not just a case of post-honeymoon disillusionment, excitement wearing off, or partners no longer being on their best behavior. It's the familiar patterns of childhood surfacing, which we don't yet have the strength or understanding to recognize and resist. So our in-laws make ghostly appearances, and we no longer recognize the person we married. We both start acting more like our parents than like ourselves.

Compliance and identification are at the root of many other transgressions which spoil relationships. For example, promiscuous behavior (when not caused by early sexual abuse) is often based either on identification with a promiscuous parent, a compliant need not to threaten parents in an unhappy marriage by having a happier relationship, or a frustration within our own relationship because we can't be ourselves.

Every couple needs to be prepared for their compliant and identified personality parts to show up. Here is where mindful attention plays a critical role in sustaining intimacy under pressure. It allows both partners to discern and discard these dysfunctional, self-betraying behaviors, and to stay present with the one we love.

STEP 2. TALKING SO OTHERS REALLY HEAR YOU

In Step 1, we explored the world of feelings and the drawbacks of hiding them. Since our feelings are an important part of who we are, not having or not expressing them keeps others from knowing us intimately.

And we need to express feelings appropriately. If we don't, we're likely to get blindsided and act them out in hurtful and damaging ways instead. Not to directly communicate how we feel can strain any relationship to its limits. We discussed earlier how withholding feelings can also cause our own physical and emotional illness. One expert in family therapy issues, Dale Larsen, put it succinctly:

> You've heard the expression, "You're only as sick as your secrets"? Well, in fact, people who keep troubling information to themselves report a greater incidence of depression, anxiety and physical ailments, like severe aches and pains, colds, poor appetite, weight changes and fatigue. The symptoms result from the stress of having and concealing painful or embarrassing information.[56]

One manifestation of the strain poor communication puts on relationships is sometimes called the "Seven Year Itch." The wandering eyes and love affairs that characterize this crisis are the result of a serious backlog of unspoken thoughts and feelings. Love seems dead at home and so is sought elsewhere. But love can be revivified by clearing the air and reopening communication.

Similarly, in dating situations we may think the initial excitement has gone away after a few weeks, but what has really happened is that we've not fully communicated and have inadvertently created distance by our withholding. Finding a new flame will result in the same brief cycle of excitement followed by bore-dom unless we learn to keep showing up fully in relationship.

The inability to talk about one's feelings is behind many dys-functional patterns in relationships, from distance between part-ners to blaming to emotionally escalating arguments.

Poor communication can even result in spousal abuse. The frustration of not knowing how to please one's partner can build to the extent that it finally gets expressed physically. Here's how this might look:

John was easily frustrated. He married Betty, who identified with her martyred mother. By no accident these two people found each other. They came to therapy after their verbal fights had escalated to physical violence, which had scared both of them. In therapy Betty learned to say more clearly what she wanted and needed from John and to set clear limits about the language she would and would not tolerate.

John, not having had empathic role models, was surprised to hear Betty had unmet needs and had no idea she felt as frus-trated as he about not getting them met. Although this couple was in touch with their anger and frustration, they didn't know how to talk about their feelings without getting into arguments. Each said too little, and when they did talk to each other, their requests were filled with blame and accusation instead of direct statements of what it was they weren't getting or were getting too much of. John would say things like, "You can't even fix food the way I like it. What are you, some kind of princess that doesn't cook?"

Betty would feel so angry and defensive she wouldn't even ask what kind of food John wanted, so it remained a mystery. It never occurred to her to say something like this: When you accuse me of such terrible things, I feel so defensive and awful I imagine you don't love me and just should hire a cook. Besides, I don't even want to know what you like. I'm sure I could make the foods you like if you'd just tell me nicely what they were."

John wasn't aware he'd never told her what he liked. They both felt perpetually frustrated and angry simply because they didn't know how to get across to each other what they wanted. Their relationship took a radical turn for the better once they learned what the problem was and how to speak to each other respectfully.

* * *

Another example is the case of Joanie and Stan. They had been seeing each other on and off for years, with brief periods of living together. The brevity was due to Stan's inability to share his thoughts and feelings about his relationship with Joanie without being offensive. The words he chose always came out wrong, misrepresented his intentions and hurt her. Then, in awkward attempts to make things better, he made them worse. Close quarters intensified the problem, so they found it less stressful to live apart.

As this couple talked about their issues, we learned that both of them had been tyrannized by explosively angry fathers. Joanie re-experienced the trauma whenever Stan got angry, and Stan's anger compensated for his own sensitivity, which his father had severely criticized. Now Stan got to be the "strong" one. Whenever he felt deeply moved, he found something to get angry about to hide his softer emotion. The sensitivity he criticized in Joanie was a disowned, or "shadow" quality in himself.

Sometimes the problem is less our ability to communicate than reluctance due to the fear of possible repercussions. The stakes feel dangerously high when the information we have could turn someone special away if we chose to share it. This gets particularly complicated when moral issues are involved.

For example, one client, a single male about thirty-eight years old, told us the following story:

I'd been dating Martha for about seven months pretty steadily. She wasn't seeing anybody else, but I didn't want to be monogamous, although for the most part I was.

Anyway, while she was visiting her family in southern California, I was invited to a party. I met someone there. It was one of those wild chance things, not like I really cared about her or anything. We had sex and she gave me the clap. By the time Martha got back a week or so later, I already had symptoms. I went to the doctor but didn't want to tell her, so I avoided sex for a few days while I took the medicine. She didn't catch on, but I felt nervous. She kept asking, "What's the matter, what's wrong with you?" What was I supposed to say?

I probably could have gotten away with it, but I started to feel guilty. I wanted to own up, but I was scared she'd leave me. When I finally told her the truth, she got angry, then cried. But then she said she was relieved! She'd thought I was going to leave her! That surprised the heck out of me. I haven't messed around since then. Martha's too good. It just isn't worth it.

No matter how scared we are, in the long run withholding is much more destructive to the relationship. And it's important to talk about even the tiniest of annoyances. Nothing is too petty to mention. Important issues that remain hidden or unresolved erect walls of distance between us and significant others.

HOW TO EXPRESS PRACTICALLY ANYTHING

Old school communication tends to let sleeping dogs lie: "I could have gone on perfectly well without ever hearing that!" But withholding whatever's struck in the craw has consequences. It's more in the service of authenticity to err on the side of disclosure than to withhold. But how do we reveal difficult thoughts and emotions so that others can hear us without feeling judged, criticized or otherwise devastated?

First we should explore, accept, and own our discomfort. Very few issues are totally one-sided. If we can take responsibility for our part in whatever troubles us and stop being self-defensive about it, we'll be less apt to blame, judge and ascribe the problem to someone or something else, as in: "She made me angry."

It may be hard to sort out, but no one really makes us feel anything. That we feel angry (or whatever we feel) is our experience and our responsibility. We just need appropriate ways to communicate about it. The model we've found most useful is the "I message" technique, popularized years ago by Dr. Thomas Gordon.[57] He used three elements in his model: what happened, how one felt about it, and what one wanted or needed – fact, feeling, and favor. We added a fourth – "The Fantasy."

In our model, which we call 'using the four F's,' the "I" statement has those four parts, in the following order:

1. *The Fact:* what happened, just the facts (objective).

2. *The Feeling:* the emotion or subjective response I had.

3. *The Fantasy:* what I imagined you must be thinking or feeling to have treated me the way you did; the MGM production that went on in my head.

4. *The Favor:* what I want or need from you.

Put into a sentence, it looks like this:

"When you did _____ *(concisely state the facts)*, (or "When 'X' happened _____)

I felt _____ *(state the feeling or feelings here)*.

I imagined _____ *(state the fantasy here)*

and what I would like /need from you is _____ *(state the favor here)*."

For example:

(1) "When you came home late and hadn't let me know ahead of time, (2) I felt hurt, angry and disappointed. (3) I imagined you didn't care about me. (4) What I want from you is to know you care, and I'd like you to let me know when your plans change."

Here is another example:

(1) "When I worked really hard to do a good job on this project and you didn't say anything, (2) I felt frustrated and unappreciated. (3) I imagined you didn't even notice. (4) What I would like from you is some recognition."

For an effective "I-statement" using the 'four F' model,' all four elements need to be included. This is an exercise, a technique. People don't really talk this way under ordinary circumstances, especially under pressure. Both people need to understand and accept the model and agree to use it for this to work. Frankly, once you've done this a couple of times it gets a lot easier and the fact that it works is self-reinforcing. But without a model like this, which includes the four necessary elements of communication, people go around in circles, caught in a whirlwind of escalating frustration and anger that can erode trust and intimacy.

If, for instance, I use the 4-F's model instead of blaming someone for something, my partner-in-argument gets it immediately that I am coming from a place of love, concern, and reparation. S/he won't feel defensive anymore listening to what I have to say, and s/he can attend instead to my concern.

We're convinced from our clinical as well as our personal experience, that the vast majority of relationship issues can be resolved through authentic communication.

Here is an example of how we used the 4-F's model. If, for instance, I use the model to help clarify a couple's deep conflict that threatened to break up their relationship:

Belinda and Ray's were engaged but deeply troubled. Years ago, Belinda had tattooed an old boyfriend's name on her shoulder. At first, Ray joked about it, but it began to really bother him. She promised him she'd get it removed, but kept delaying despite his repeated requests. At first Ray made light of it, but as time went on he got more and more upset. His anger made Belinda withdraw and distance herself. Finally Ray said he couldn't take it anymore. That's when they came to therapy. We asked them to use I-statements to help each other understand what the other was going through and explained the 4-F's model. Here's how they used it:

Belinda: When you make fun of me or take lightly what I take seriously, I feel humiliated. I imagine you have no idea how it makes me feel and I would like you not to do it.

Ray: When you go into your shell, I feel hurt, sad, rejected and afraid you'll leave me. I imagine you don't know how deeply it affects me. If you have to do that, I want you to reassure me that you still love me and are there for me.

Belinda: When you yell at me and persistently nag me to do something I already agreed to do, I resent it. I feel disappointed and physically afraid. I imagine you don't trust me and will always be on my back about something. I need to be sure you can control your temper and that you still trust and love me.

The pain and love they both felt was so clearly expressed that the tension in the room melted away, and the stage was set for healing.

We should mention that an I-statement exercise involves more than just an I-statement. During the session, each I-statement quoted above was followed by considerable discussion before we moved on to the next one.

Despite their power, there are two situations when the use of "I-statements" alone won't do the trick. The first is when the relationship is truly a mismatch. Couples who quite simply have made a mistake in getting together will eventually discover this. Authentic communication can't fix the truly broken, but it can speed up the discovery process. The second instance is when one person has a hidden agenda s/he isn't willing or feels unable to disclose or resolve. Until the unspoken has at last seen the light of day, one-sided attempts at authentic communication will falter and fail.

***

A MISMATCHED COUPLE

David and Erica met in graduate school. They were the same age, studying for the same advanced degree, and got to know each other well before dating. They genuinely liked each other and both felt excited by the possibilities in their relationship. The problem they faced was not the usual kind of incompatibility.

Although both of them were graduate students in Psychology, Erica had been a meditator and had seen a therapist for several years. She was active in the Women's Movement and had taken a number of personal growth workshops, all of which had made profound changes in her worldview and ways of relating to other people. David was a kind, generous, and sensitive man.. He was in touch with his feelings and didn't believe he had to prove his manhood to anyone. However, he'd not done much inner work: he'd never been in counseling/psychotherapy nor resolved his old childhood issues.

At first their relationship blossomed. Erica pointed out psychological issues to David through her insight, while David's masculine gentility was healing for her. But as time went on, Erica began to feel more like a mentor than a lover. She began to resent the time and energy she had to spend helping David understand what was clear as day for her. It was as if she had to put her personal goals on hold in order to help him catch up with her.

Because they were both able and willing to talk authentically about these issues as they came up, they both knew a crisis was pending, so when it finally hit there weren't any major surprises. Erica simply had to move on. David understood it but couldn't accept it. Although they were no longer dating, he held on to the hope of reconciliation for months. Finally, one evening he called her and poured out his feelings. She heard him out, then said,

"Dave, I know how you feel, and in many ways it hasn't been easy for me either. I care about you a lot. I appreciate many things about you, but there's isn't anything I can do."

Although David didn't like hearing this finality, Erica's feedback was clean and clear. Her message hurt, but it validated him and expressed her genuine feeling for him at the same time. After this conversation he could let go and get on with his life.

HIDDEN AGENDAS

Hidden agendas warrant some further attention. In most conversations, there is something at stake. The higher the stakes, the more heated the conversation. Sometimes a considerable amount of heat can be generated over seemingly nothing, and despite the fire and brimstone, virtually nothing gets resolved. We're mystified and upset, arguing all the time, getting nowhere. What on Earth is going on?

This is a sure-fire sign of a hidden agenda. Underneath issues like who should take out the garbage may be strongly held beliefs, attitudes, positions, and values that feel non-negotiable. They reflect our conditioning, or beliefs arising out of our conditioning. These powerful and often toxic but deeply-held convictions underlie and pervade our conscious thought, making it nearly impossible to be vulnerable and get to the bottom of what's really going on. These are hidden agendas.

For example, Brian felt his wife, Jean, had something against occasionally visiting his parents, although she claimed she was just too busy and encouraged him to go alone. Since seeing his parents with her was important to Brian's family values, he began to feel she didn't care about his feelings. When it came time to plan their vacation, Jean wanted to go to the beach, but Brian insisted they go to the mountains and drop in for a day or two to see his parents, who lived in that direction. Jean agreed, partially allaying Brian's concerns, but she felt resentful, believing he thought her needs less important than his. Since each was afraid of confrontation, neither spoke directly about this.

Although Brian *felt* unloved and Jean *felt* powerless, neither expressed these feelings to the other. As long as they kept these feelings inside, the hidden agendas remained and continued to influence their feelings and perceptions.

GARDEN VARIETY HIDDEN AGENDAS

Insecurity, and the need for reassurance about love and trust, is a common hidden agenda. In fact, according to psychologist Karl Albrecht, the fear of abandonment is one of the five basic fears from which all other fears arise. [The other four are extinction, mutilation, loss of autonomy, and what he calls 'ego-death.']⁵⁸ Just about everyone, at some point, comes up against this terrible core doubt and fully expects their partner to be secretly planning an escape. The funny part is, our partner is usually afraid *we'll* abandon *them*. The only way to deal with the bogeyman is face it head on, to surface the hidden agenda. Anytime we worry our partner is dissatisfied or about to leave, we can discuss it: "I'm having this fantasy you're upset or displeased with me. Is there any truth to this?" Or, "I imagine you're thinking of leaving me. I need a reality check. Is it true?" Then we get everything out in the open. If our partner is dissatisfied, at least we can find out why, and we can probably resolve the problem.

Related to hidden agendas is covert hostility or resentment. They are hidden, but their effect is felt. We may catch ourselves wanting to lash out or make a sarcastic remark, but we restrain ourselves from saying it. Instead the cutting remarks go on inside our head. If we don't talk about what we're experiencing, our resentment or hostility will leak out in a tone of voice or attitude. Our partner will feel our negativity no matter how polite our words. And the inner hostility is usually a symptom signaling a whole set of feelings we've stuffed in our emotional closet that need to be talked about.

If we don't get clear about subtle feelings, they create an undercurrent. Hidden feelings or agendas were likened by psychologist Will Schutz to bowling balls under the table. His analogy goes like this: Joseph and Joanne went on vacation to a mountain resort. During their games of table tennis all appeared to be having a great time. But under the table were bowling balls rolling, breaking legs.[59]

Hidden agendas are unexpressed values, needs, hopes, desires (including negative desires, like vengeance or wanting to use, take advantage, or get the better of someone) that are assumed to be out of reach or unacceptable in some way, and therefore intentionally kept secret. They may also be so much a part of our conditioning that we aren't aware of them until they are challenged. Since we can't (or won't) talk about them directly, we try to get them met indirectly or covertly instead, as in the case of Brian and Jean.

Hidden agendas attached to old conditioning are tenacious and self-reinforcing, still with us years later. This is because they are survival-based. We developed them to make sense of experience in general, but in particular, difficult and traumatic experiences. Today they continue to act as a filter on our experience and we re-work our perceptions, easily misinterpreting, and distorting information to fit them. We let in evidence that supports our view or position, and filter out what doesn't fit. This continues unabated until we become aware of what's really at stake and trace the issues back to the beliefs that generated them in the first place.

Until the underlying beliefs are dispelled, the positions, hopes, needs, and even values based on those beliefs will continue to be frustrated, challenged, and disrespected, but no amount of discussion and arguing will ever settle the matter.

HOW TO RECOGNIZE A HIDDEN AGENDA

There are three basic dimensions to hidden agendas, and different ways these show up between people.

The basic issues are (1) power or control (my needs are less important than yours; I have less influence /status than you do); (2) caring or interest (you're not interested in me anymore; you don't care about me they way you used to); and (3) attractiveness (you don't find me attractive anymore; you find others more attractive than me).

Hidden agendas manifest in several different ways. The most common type is when the person is frustrated in getting what s/he wants but has a covert plan for getting it. For example, Joanne needs money to buy some earrings but believes her husband doesn't care enough to give it to her. So she asks for gas money and goes shopping instead.

Another common type results in less devious behavior, but it's more painful. This is when one party despairs of being heard or having his needs or desires respected or attended to and has no strategies to get satisfaction. For example, Jean didn't feel she could influence her husband so she accompanied him on their vacation with a "grin and bear it, but I'll get even later" attitude. This is a power issue. The one who feels powerless will feel s/he has no recourse but to comply, at least for now.

A third kind of hidden agenda is when we don't say all of what we really mean for fear of hurting or alienating our partner. We leave out one or more of the four "F's" in the 4-F's model (fact, feeling, fantasy, favor). This leaves our partner guessing what we really mean or feel. For example, Brian told Jean he thought she was being unfair not to agree to visit his parents with him. He left out how hurt he was by what he thought was her rejection of his family, and what he imagined her motives. This partial communication confused Jean, who felt he was running roughshod over her in planning the vacation.

In the following examples, the second speaker misinterprets the first speaker's words and uses this as evidence to support the concern that his/her partner doesn't care, isn't attracted, or has more power. Or the first speaker may actually have a hidden agenda and the partner guesses at it.

He: "I thought you gave that dress to the Goodwill."

She: "I can get one more summer out of it." She thinks: "He thinks I'm unattractive."

She: "I don't think we should get married until I finish school.

He: "But you saw what our income will be. I can handle it."

He thinks: "She doesn't want to stay with me. She's not committed to me. I was afraid of that!"

He: "I'm not going to do the dishes."

She: "Never mind. I'll do them."

She thinks: "His needs are more important than mine."

She: "I'm tired tonight. I'd rather not have sex."

He: "It's been a hard week."

He thinks: "She doesn't care about me."

He: "Oh, I'm sorry. I guess I wasn't listening. I've got a lot on my mind."

She: "Well, what I said was. . ."

She thinks: "He's not interested in me."

Hidden agendas are hard to spot. Only the clues tip us off. What are the clues? First of all, conversations with a hidden agenda keep cycling over and over the same issue without reaching resolution. This can be a relatively minor issue which you'd think two intelligent adults could settle easily. But instead of resolution one gets more conflict. Instead of feeling relief, we feel increasingly angry or frustrated. When this occurs, we can suspect that we're in the grip of a hidden agenda

Here are some other clues:

1. Feeling lonely when talking to my partner about certain things.

2. Feeling more like being alone or with someone else than with him/her.

3. Feeling judged, criticized, excluded or ignored by him/her.

4. Imagining my partner is neither interested in nor responsive to me.

5. Feeling moody.

Sometimes both people in a relationship have a hidden agenda. We can suspect this is the case if the following are true:

1. There are some definite taboo subjects in the relationship that are never discussed, by mutual agreement, spoken or not.

2. There are secrets that carry a high emotional charge and a fear that revealing them will hurt the other person.[60]

3. One partner keeps silent his disagreement or disapproval of his partner's behavior he doesn't like.

Hidden agendas, whenever we realize we're involved in one, should be investigated and brought to light. As soon as partners stop putting up with silence, indifference, and camouflage and insist upon complete communication, tensions clear up. We need to be alert to the clues and diligently follow them up.

Sometimes we may believe we've uncovered a hidden agenda while we're in an arguing mode. This can be deceptive. When we're in the midst of an argument, we're probably not stating our true feelings accurately. Then it's best to take a break to cool off and start again using "I-statements."

Once we've clarified hidden agendas behind an unresolved issue, the next step is to negotiate an agreement that satisfies both partners. Change is now possible, but if one person feels justified and the other feels blamed, this may start another round of fighting. In most cases, both people's positions need to change, at least a little. The hard truth is that we can't pry someone loose from a problematic hidden agenda, even one that's been brought to light and discussed, unless we first acknowledge our part in the problem. When it's a clear two-way street, the other person will be more willing to change. This is true especially if I let him/her know what I would like and state it as a wish, not a demand. In other words, my responsibility is to myself and to the relationship, and any attempts I make to try to change or control you to solve my problems won't go far and are likely to backfire.

As long as agendas remain hidden, be it for days, weeks or even years, they will muddy the waters and hinder all efforts to problem-solve.

Unmet needs, complicated by hidden agendas, crop up even in the most compatible relationships. When they do, they (and the sometimes desperate clues people leave to signal there's something wrong), should never be ignored. The underlying issues may only be minor annoyances, but they are more likely just the top level of a whole sack of grievances. One person we know played tragic love songs on the piano, like "Love for Sale," within earshot of her husband. This was her way of hinting she was falling out of love with him. She couldn't talk about it. Her husband, not one to take a hint, never did get the message. This is a good example of how futile it is to assume our partner can mind-read.

The point is, people go to great lengths to alert their partners that something is wrong, and if they can't say it outright, they'll leave clues. Non-verbal behavior, like tone of voice and facial expression, hints and indirect suggestions are clues. In Step 3 we talk more about how to respond to them. Briefly put, hidden agendas can only be cleared up in one way: by getting them out on the table. By definition, once a hidden agenda is brought to light, it loses its destructive power. So the moment we feel unloved, abandoned or manipulated, we should stop everything and talk about it.

HOW NOT TO COMMUNICATE

There's an old saying that one can't not communicate, however, there are some surefire ways to make another person feel defensive or angry. They include the following[61]:

Ordering	Advising
Warning	Criticizing
Moralizing	Name-Calling
Judging	Teaching
Shaming	Commanding
Diagnosing	Preaching
Psychoanalyzing	Blaming
Directing	Ridiculing
Threatening	Instructing
	Giving
	Suggestions

Most of these are obvious, although advising and giving suggestions may not at first glance seem offensive. These are often considered positive, supportive forms of communication. In fact, they're not, unless asked for. If someone doesn't ask you to help them solve their problem and you volunteer to undertake the project, your helpfulness will be perceived as invasive and irritating even if you get a polite response. For some of us over forty types it may seem unduly harsh to say don't give unsolicited help, especially if being helpful was an important childhood way of winning brownie points with a parent. But say it we must. If you must give something, give the benefit of the doubt. The other person will ask for help or advice if he or she needs it. And if you must say something, simply ask if you can be of help in some way. This simple question conveys the kind of respect and support everyone appreciates.

EXERCISES

These exercises are to assess your awareness of the common obstacles mentioned above. Evaluate yourself in general on a scale of 1 - 10, with 10 being the highest mark for refraining from using these methods.

1. Since we all occasionally communicate less than skillfully, write down one or two recent conversations when you were judgmental and blaming. Quote yourself as accurately as possible. Then write down an alternative to what you said, using an 4-F's model I-statement.

2. What might have changed had you responded nonjudgmentally?

3. List people from your past who used effective and ineffective communication styles.

4. Whose communication styles do you find yourself using? Occasionally? Frequently?

5. How would you rate yourself as a communicator, over all? Try to describe your style and give yourself a rating on a 1-10 scale, with 10 being the highest score.

6. Ask some friends how they would rate you as a communicator. Compare this with your own evaluation in question #5, and use this feedback to make the changes you'd like to see in your communication style.

This chapter has been about creating intimacy through authentic communication, which is the primary way connect with other people. We're convinced that most of the problems people have with each other are due to misunderstandings or misperceptions, which accurate and complete communication clears up. As difficult as it is to make new habits, no efforts a person makes to improve his communication style are ever in vain.

"Trying to be better, is to be better."
~ American actress Charlotte Cushman

But outward expression is only half the process. Listening is just as important, and to this we next turn our attention.

STEP 3. LISTENING AND THE POWER OF SILENCE

Listening, the receptive side of the communication process, is problematic because it requires silence, and many of us are uncomfortable with silence. We leap in to fill it or fix it, to soothe our fears of being a poor conversationalist, or to help out someone who seems at a loss for words. But if we leap in, we don't leave any room for those of us who need a little extra space to come forth with ideas and feelings. How many times have the introverts among us chosen to remain silent in a group of extroverts, friends or otherwise, rather than force our way in or court ridicule by asking people to wait while we take a moment to reflect before speaking?

Adding to the discomfort of silence is the "feeling phobia" we discussed earlier. Since silence gives room for feelings to well up, we may try to avoid or suppress them by chatter, joking or verbal competitiveness. Choosing silence over anxious chatter leans on the side of authenticity every time.

If we're bothered by someone who is very talkative and we know them well enough, we can say, "You seem to have a lot of energy today. You're talking a blue streak. Are you feeling anything uncomfortable?" This gives them space to get in touch with whatever anxiety is propelling their chatter.

Silence is truly golden. Within the context of a conversation, it's more often a sign of respect than of stupidity or dullness. It's a way of honoring the other person's process, of indicating that we not only believe their thoughts are valuable, but that they personally are worth our time and attention.

M. Scott Peck gives a good illustration of the quality attention we give when silent:

Not very long ago I attended a lecture by a famous man on an aspect of the relationship between psychology and religion in which I have long been interested. Because of my interest I had a certain amount of expertise in the subject and immediately recognized the lecturer to be a great sage indeed. I also sensed love in the tremendous effort he was exerting to communicate, with all manner of examples, highly abstract concepts that were difficult for us, his audience, to comprehend. I therefore listened to him with all the intentness of which I was capable. Throughout the hour and a half he talked, sweat was literally dripping down my face in the air-conditioned auditorium. By the time he was finished I had a throbbing headache, the muscles in my neck were rigid from my effort at concentration, and I felt completely drained and exhausted.

Although I estimated that I'd understood no more than 50% of what this great man had said, I was amazed by the large number of brilliant insights he'd given me. Following the lecture, which was well attended by culture-seeking individuals, I wandered about through the audience listening to their comments. Generally they were disappointed. Knowing his reputation, they had expected more. They found him hard to follow and his talk confusing. He was not as competent a speaker as they had hoped to hear.

In contradistinction to the others, I was able to hear much of what this great man said, precisely because I was willing to do the work of listening to him.[62]

Quality listening is generally not so arduous in normal conversation. What matters is that by giving full attention while keeping an open mind despite whatever contrary opinions we may hold, we open ourselves to many gifts, such as the trust and confidence placed in us by another person who feels safe and able to be him/herself in our presence.

Few of us practice "empty mind" listening. Most of us go into a conversation with our assumptions or inferences in full force. These become our screen for finding evidence to prove our assumptions. We don't actually tune in to the subtleties of what's being said. We may even strike an attitude of superiority, feel put upon, hostile or fearful. We'll interact more with our fantasy than with the person speaking to us.

An example is the following story related by Stephen R. Covey. It took place on a subway in New York one Sunday morning:

People were sitting quietly – some reading newspapers, some lost in thought, some resting with their eyes closed. It was a calm, peaceful scene.

Then suddenly, a man and his children entered the subway car. The children were so loud and rambunctious that instantly the whole climate changed.

The man sat down next to me and closed his eyes, apparently oblivious to the situation. The children were yelling back and forth, throwing things, even grabbing people's papers. It was very disturbing. And yet, the man sitting next to me did nothing.

It was difficult not to feel irritated. I couldn't believe he could be so insensitive as to let his children run wild and do nothing about it, taking no responsibility at all. It was easy to see that everyone else on the subway felt irritated, too. So finally, with what I felt was unusual patience and restraint, I turned to him and said, "Sir, your children are really disturbing a lot of people. I wonder if you couldn't control them a little more?"

The man lifted his gaze as if to come to a conscious-ness of the situation for the first time and said softly, "Oh, you're right. I guess I should do something about it. We just came from the hospital where their mother died about an hour ago. I don't know what to think, and I guess they don't know how to handle it either."

Can you imagine what I felt at that moment? Suddenly I saw things differently, and because I saw differently, I thought differently, I felt differently, I behaved dif-ferently. My irritation vanished. I didn't have to worry about controlling my attitude or my behavior; my heart was filled with the man's pain. Feelings of sympathy and compassion flowed freely. "Your wife just died? Oh, I'm so sorry! Can you tell me about it? What can I do to help?" Everything changed in an instant.[63]

The more we can empty our minds of judgmental attitudes and replace them with humility and compassion, the better chance we have of understanding another person's reality.

* * *

Here's another example of how judgments distort our perception. A woman we know attended a single's party in San Francisco. As she pulled into the parking lot, she saw a handsome man getting out of a pickup truck that had an American flag flying from the right front fender. Automatically a stereotype came to mind, and she thought to herself, "Redneck." At the same time she couldn't help noticing the driver seemed to be her type. After she got out of her car, she gave the truck a once-over, just to give him another chance. Now she saw on the left rear bumper a couple of stickers that offended her: one for the National Rifle Association, and another that read, "Due to the shortage of wood and paper products, wipe your butt on a spotted owl."

"Well, that confirms it," she thought. "Trouble! This isn't a person I want to be with."

During the party, however, she noticed her friend, Jeannie spending a lot of time with this fellow and acting all excited about going out with him the next weekend.

"Jeannie!" she cried in dismay, "You don't know this guy. You should have seen what he drove up in!"

"Oh that!" she laughed. "He almost didn't make it to the party. Couldn't get his car started. He had to borrow his neighbor's truck!"

* * *

Not only had her judgments done this man an injustice, they had stopped her from listening to her heart and deprived her of a romantic opportunity.

If we do end up in conversation with someone we judge, the person being judged senses it on some level, feels uncomfortable and/or defensive and has a harder time revealing him/herself.

Take the case of Ernie. He had an initial business meeting with a prospective client. His wife met that same client later in the day without knowing what her husband had said to him. When she told Ernie of the chance meeting and conversation, he questioned her: "Oh really? What did you tell him?"

It wasn't the words so much as his tone of voice that set her on edge and made her feel defensive without knowing why. She felt guilty without any conscious reason for it and wanted to evade a direct answer. Until they discussed these feelings, their communication was strained.

A common block to our ability to listen is wanting to prescribe for others what to do or how to be. The temptation is to assume that what worked for us must be good for someone else. Unless we can listen closely, with an empty mind, without judgment or opinion, our ego can get in the way and we won't be able to hear what they're really saying.

For instance, a person may feel superior about his advanced degree from the school of hard knocks and as a result offers patronizing advice to his partner. The partner bristles with defensiveness at this presumption and rightfully refuses the advice on how to live his life. However, in a case where one person sees a threat the other person does not see, it's worth risking someone's annoyance. In a situation like that, unasked for advice could be life-saving.

There's a myth that once couples feel really close or have been together a long time, that they know each other well enough to finish each other's sentences. Actually, few things are more annoying than someone "guessing" what you're going to say because they think they know and want to save some of their own precious time. Bullocks! Everybody should have the right to say what they want to say. This nasty habit may seem well intentioned, and sometimes is, but can also be disguised impatience, disrespect, or in some cases outright intimidation. It can even influence the other person to say what you expect them to, or even to drop the whole thing.

Silence shows we value the other person. It's also a form of vulnerability. To quietly listen to someone while they look us straight in the eye and say, "I love you" can be profound, ecstatic, or terrifying.

Choosing silence over anxious chatter leans on the side of authenticity. How might this work when facing an angry person and being confronted with high energy and strong feelings? How do we listen respectfully?

If a person's anger is escalating and we feel endangered, healthy communication probably isn't possible. If we can't defuse the anger, we need to protect ourselves, by leaving the situation or getting help. However, when someone is angry and we do not feel threatened, it is respectful to be quiet and listen carefully to find out exactly what's going on. At some point we can ask questions, but usually the person will tell us, especially if s/he thinks we're to blame. We should bite our tongue and listen without arguing, defending or judging, no matter how defensive we may feel inside. As a result, when it's our turn to speak, the other person should by that time feel listened to and be quite willing to reciprocate by listening to what we have to say.

For example, I received a phone call from an angry and seriously ill man in a support group I also attend. He called to rail at me for something he thought was my fault and had a full head of steam up. Although I knew I was not the guilty party, I also knew how important the issue was to him. But he seemed to get angrier as he spoke. Finally I had to interrupt him. "Brad, stop yelling at me!" I had to raise my voice to be heard over him, but immediately lowered it again. "I can tell you the history of this problem and who we should talk to about it." I went on to acknowledge what he had said, explained what I knew and suggested whom to contact. His attitude changed immediately. He spoke calmly about a couple of more things, thanked me and hung up.

In a court of law, silence in the face of accusation may signal guilt, but that's not true in everyday conversation. Listening respectfully is not the same as accepting blame, even if we deserve it. Recognizing another person's feelings and showing our willingness to hear whatever they have to say is light years away from an admission of guilt. It gives both parties time: for the one to vent his feelings, and for the other to get some perspective by listening and then respond accurately and empathically.

Every now and then we run into a a chronic complainer. I remember getting calls from such people during all-night shifts at a hot line where I volunteered. These people, in their neediness, glom onto a sympathetic ear and hold on, trying to make us feel guilty if we tune out or try to end the conversation. If someone is complaining rather than seeking solutions to their problems, we're being exploited as sponges for their anxiety and we need to extricate ourselves. After listening long enough to figure out that complaining is all the person is doing, I used to say, "It sounds like this is a difficult time for you. I'm sorry to hear that and I'll have to hang up in five minutes." Then two or three minutes later I'd say something like that again, and when we reached the five minute mark, I'd say goodbye, usually hanging up on them mid-sentence. I was kind, but to the point. In a situation like this there is not much to be done but listen well, be empathic, set a limit, and then follow through on it. .

NON-VERBAL COMMUNICATION

One way to show our interest and let others know how receptive and interested we are in what they have to say is through non-verbal communication.

A well known 1968 psychological study reported that communication is 93% non-verbal.[64] This idea has been around a long time. A proverb from ancient China warns against the person whose stomach doesn't move when he laughs,[65] and the Bible says, "The show of their countenance doth witness against them."[66] The ten major non-verbal indicators and what they indicate are summarized in the following table:

INDICATORS OF NON-VERBAL COMMUNICATION

INDICATOR	*WARM/ WELCOMING*	*COLD/ ALIENATING*
Tone of voice	Soft	Hard
Facial expression	Smiling, interested	Poker-faced, frowning, disinterested
Posture	Leaning toward the other, relaxed	Leaning away from the other, tense
Eye contact	Looking into the other's eyes	Avoidance of eye contact
Touching	Touch the other softly	Avoid touching
Gestures	Open, welcoming	Closed, guarded
Spatial distance	Close	Distant
Clothing	Neat, clean, color-ful, tasteful	Disheveled, dirty, discordant
Grooming, hygiene	Neat, clean	Unkempt, poor hygiene
Environment	Open, good light and air, clean, orderly	Claustrophobic, chaotic, dirty

ACTIVE LISTENING

Active listening is a time-honored communication tool used to insure that messages have been delivered and received accurately. However, this requires staying in touch with our own feelings at the same time, without tuning the other person out. Authenticity demands this "divided attention," because if we ignore our own spontaneous thoughts that inevitably occur as we listen, we run the risk of unintentionally biasing ourselves against what is being said because of our own ingrained opinions and judgments. We have to stay aware of our own thoughts, in order to listen well. This is a little different from "empty mind" listening. "Empty mind" is the way to begin listening – making sure we are not coming into a conversation with prejudices and an agenda all in place. But during the conversation, we need to be aware of thoughts that arise in us in response to what the other person is saying.

The formal origins for active listening were in the client centered...etc therapy of Dr. Carl Rogers, and widely popularized in the "Effectiveness Training" books by Dr. Thomas Gordon. According to Dr. Gordon,

> [A person using active listening...] tries to understand... tries to understand the sender's feelings or what the sender means. He puts that understanding in his own words and feeds it back for verification. He doesn't send any message of his own, such as evaluation, opinion, advice, logic analysis or a question. He feeds back *only what he feels the sender's message meant*, nothing more, nothing less.[67]

He goes on to say that using the technique of active listening allows the other person

> ...to say more, to go deeper, to develop her thoughts further, to redefine the problem on her own and then tentatively develop some insights about herself and make a good start towards solving her own problem.[68]

Active listening is a style of communication which elicits maximum information, enhances the speaker's self esteem, creates a sense of emotional safety, supports the speaker to come forth with more of his or her personal truth, and honors the relationship itself. As listeners we use five basic techniques to accomplish this:

1. Encouraging – which conveys our interest and support.

2. Clarifying – which helps us get more (and more accurate) information.

3. Restating – which shows we're listening and understanding correctly and acts as a reality check on what we think we heard.

4. Reflecting – saying back to the speaker what we heard him say – which shows we're listening and understanding not only what speaker is saying but also how he feels. It also helps us evaluate our own feelings and impact as a communicator when we hear our own ideas expressed by someone else.

5. Summarizing – which reviews basic ideas, pulls together

important ideas and facts, and establishes the basis for further discussion.

Here's an example of active listening:

Rhonda and Warner are spending a day in the countryside. In the middle of a walk in the woods, Rhonda suddenly starts to cry. They stop walking. Warner is concerned and immediately wonders if there's something he did or said. "Rhonda, what's wrong?" he asks in a caring tone of voice.

Rhonda responds to this invitation by saying, "I don't know. I was feeling so happy, then suddenly I'm crying and I can't stop."

Warner doesn't have much to go on yet, so he does the only supportive thing he can. He feeds back what he heard with something like, "You were happy and now you're crying." This keeps the door open for Rhonda to say more if she wants to. "Yeah," she replies, trying to laugh but being unable to. "I'm sorry."

Warner, paying close attention, sees that she can't laugh and hears that she feels embarrassed and apologetic. He says, "There's nothing to be sorry for. Maybe you're feeling sad about something." Then he takes care of his initial fear by asking directly, "Is it something I said or did?"

"No, it's not about you. I think it's about this place." Rhonda is still testing the water to see if it's safe to show her deeper feelings in front of him, and Warner, knowing he's not to blame, now feels safe enough to encourage her further. He says, "There's something about this place that upsets you? Do you want to talk about it?"

By actively listening, Warner communicated that he understood what Rhonda said, supported her having her feelings, and wasn't judging her or trying to "make it better." At this point, Rhonda had the option to confide in him or to continue working on the problem within herself.

Let's take a closer look at how this process works. People don't always say what they mean, and there may be something else going on just under the surface.

The communication process begins with someone experiencing something and wanting to communicate about it. Sometimes it can be done clearly and directly, but if this is anything more than the transfer of technical information, feelings are usually involved, and it's not always emotionally safe to reveal them. We don't know if our feelings will be welcome. Maybe we'll get shot down.

People generally test the water first, and this testing process may be connected to an opportunity for some very deep healing. So, before looking more closely at Rhonda and Warner's communication, we want to address the process of "unconscious testing."

One of the principles underlying much of what we've written here is the well-researched idea that certain mental tasks, such as planning and even carrying out our plans, can be done unconsciously.[69]

One of these unconscious tasks is the attempt to disconfirm those old unconscious beliefs we discussed in Chapter 2, beliefs that may have been holding us back for years. Depending on what belief we're working on, and how we go about testing it, the person on the receiving end may have a hard time. But even difficult tests can be passed if we're aware of what's going on. The purpose of this little diversion is to alert you about testing, because it's something we all do. It's important to remember that when it happens, it's not a personal attack, nor is it a signal that the relationship is in trouble.

There are two kinds of unconscious tests. To set the scene, let's say you and I are dating and I am the tester. My story is that when I was young, both my parents often spoke sarcastically to me, putting me down, making me feel bad about myself. Over time I bought into this and my low self-esteem made me feel even more awkward than my friends probably did when it came to socializing and especially with dating. In this case, my unconscious plan is to overcome my sense of inferiority and be more free and easy with people.

The first kind of unconscious test is called a "transference" test because I'm "transferring" the old situation with my parents directly onto you. For example, if my folks put me down a lot when I wanted something badly and badgered them about it, then I'll try that with you to experience your reaction to me. Will you put me down, too? If you do, you have failed my test, my bad feelings about myself are reconfirmed, and I'm not a happy camper. But if you act kindly to my neediness, if you are supportive instead of demeaning, then you are acting differently than my parents did (and why shouldn't you, unless I happened to pick you as a girlfriend precisely because you are a sarcastic person, which might feel more comfortable and quite "normal" to me – it happens more than you think). This that goes a long way to disconfirming my old experience and helping me heal. I'll feel much more relaxed and relieved because of your more accepting response.

Transference tests are often surprising, since the old behavior being used to test your reaction may not be characteristic of your partner. If it's something benign, as in the example above, you might not even recognize it as a test. But if it's something more difficult to deal with and you recognize it in time (which we get better at with practice), then you can simply point out and ask about my behavior rather than reacting to it. You could reflect back what you heard, much as we'll see Warner do when we get back to his and Rhonda's story, as they try to get more information to help clarify the situation for each other. Asking a question also helps me return (emotionally) to the present moment and hopefully (if I've also been practicing), I'll be able to see it was something from the past and apologize if necessary. This is good news! The bad news is that the second type of unconscious test is more difficult because it feels just awful if you're on the receiving end. However, the healing potential of this kind of test is huge for the tester and is another opportunity (they are endless) for the receiver to practice mindfulness. Here's how it works:

The second kind of unconscious test is called "passive-into-active." Again, this is an attempt to re-enact an early traumatic experience that the tester feels was instrumental in the development of one of those harsh unconscious beliefs.[70]

In a passive-into-active test – and this is why it feels so bad and is more difficult to pass – I turn the tables and treat you the way I had been treated. The purpose (and remember, this is *unconscious* behavior; no one is deliberately trying to hurt you) is to see whether or not I traumatize you the same way they traumatized me.[71] The point of the test is for the tester to observe your reaction. Ideally you will not be traumatized by my sarcasm the same way I had been by my parents' sarcasm.

We, the testers (and most all of us are the testers because we nearly all have negative unconscious beliefs to contend with) learn from supportive responses, and over time, with repeated reparative experiences like this one, the old wounds eventually heal. But nobody deliberately walks into the line of fire, and that is why we usually test the "safest" possible people, namely the people we are closest to. If we are so lucky as to have a partner who is aware and willing to talk about things, we can help each other grow. When confronted with a difficult test, an authentic response to the pain, in the moment, while being compassionate to the pain of the past, cannot help but heal.

And what if we do react defensively? What if we miss an opportunity for compassion, and an argument ensues and perhaps even escalates, then what? Is all lost? Is the relationship a dead end? Not necessarily, though every relationship is different. Despite the difficulty and pain testing may cause, try to remember that the only reason the testing took place at all is because we are a loved and trusted person with whom it is safe to test. Remembering that, we can smooth our feathers to whatever extent possible, push the "reset" button, and carry on.

Now, back to Warren and Rhonda. Their *conscious* communication process looks like this:

The sender has something to communicate:

RHONDA   FEELS   SAD

The sender then tests the water by sending out a trial balloon or feeler – a statement that has his/her feelings encoded within it but which doesn't commit him/her too deeply. In other words, if the feeler isn't well-received, it can be easily withdrawn.

RHONDA FEELS   SAD,   SENDS TRIAL BALLOON

"Gee, I don't know what's wrong with me today."

Here are some other examples of trial balloons:

"Should have stayed in bed today."

"Oh, forget it."

"They said there'd be days like this."

"If it isn't one thing it's another."

"Sometimes I feel like quitting."

The main characteristic of these statements is that they can easily be turned into a joke or withdrawn without revealing our true feelings if the receiver doesn't seem open, is hostile, or if the situation isn't private enough or feels unsafe in any way. But, if the situation is safe, the trial balloon is a real invitation to communicate.

The listener, or receiver, can't really get inside the speaker's head to know his/her experience. The artful listener will not miss the true nature of the trial balloons and mistake them for small talk, but will consciously try to decode the message by inferring what the speaker feels. This is different from mind reading or making assumptions, in that we ask whether or not our inference is correct.

Dr. Gordon points out that this is just the beginning, the foundation of the problem-solving process. If I infer correctly by active listening and state my inference clearly, it's a door opener, and the speaker may feel comfortable enough to go one step further by identifying and/ or defining the real problem.

But if I can't even get the door open, there's little hope for understanding. So as a listener I send out an invitation. The most common and effective invitations are open-ended questions like,

"Would you tell me more about that?" "How did that feel?" "What was that like?"

The most skillful method, and this is the heart of active listening, is to go one step further and launch the problem-solving process immediately upon hearing a trial balloon. To do this, don't just ask an open-ended question. Open-ended questions stimulate conversation, but if time is the issue, you want to do more than that.

Instead of asking a question, get right into it by feeding back your inference about the hidden feeling:

TRIAL BALLOON,   INFERENCE,   INVITATION

(Rhonda's)   (Warner's)   (Warner's)

ELICITING RESPONSE (Rhonda's)

"I don't know. I was feeling so happy, then suddenly I'm crying and I can't stop."

(Warner infers she's embarrassed and feels apologetic. He tries to reassure, then sends an invitation.)

"That's okay. Maybe this place reminds you of something."

(Warner sends invitation eliciting response.)

"Yeah, my grandma had a summer place like this. I really miss her a lot."

Warner and Rhonda have further conversation before Warner actually sends her a more targeted invitation:

"Do you want to talk about it?

An atmosphere of openness, concern and safety has been established.

Here are some other examples:

Sender: "I don't know how I'm going to untangle this messy problem."

Inference: puzzlement, confusion

Invitation: "You're really stumped on how to solve this one."

Sender: Damn it! Why can't I get accurate blueprints out of Engineering?

Inference: anger

Invitation: "It makes you angry when you find errors in their prints."

Sender: "I'm sorry, I wasn't listening to you. I guess I'm preoccupied with a problem at home with my son. He's not doing well in school.

Inference: worry, preoccupation, anxiety

Invitation: "Sounds like you're really worried about him."

Sender: "Please, don't ask me about that now."

Inference: impatience at being interrupted

Invitation: "Sounds like you're busy right now."

Sender: "I thought the meeting today accomplished nothing."

Inference: disappointment

Invitation: "You were very disappointed with our session."[72]

In the exercises at the end of this chapter there's one to help you hone the skill of active listening. And we do need to practice. Most of us don't have much experience in giving this kind of quality attention. We may occasionally drift to another time and place, fall asleep, judge, listen to tunes in our head, etc.

SELF-LISTENING

Another barrier to listening is when we "self-listen," a term coined by Dr. Warren Farrel. Here's his definition:

> Self-listening is basically the process of catching the gist of what a person is saying and then starting to think to oneself of a similar incident which you can bring up the moment the talker takes a breath, in a way that transfers the focus of the conversation to yourself.[73]

This is one of the pitfalls of ordinary conversation and especially of active listening. Virtually everyone does it. However, we get a lot of mileage from even fledgling efforts to stop, even though it requires unaccustomed self-restraint. Others will feel closer to us because we are a safe person to be with. We "hold the space" for the other person as they contact their feelings and assess the relative safety of the situation, deciding in both conscious and unconscious ways what to do. At the same time, in this same space, we get in touch with our own feelings – those which we bring to the exchange and those which arise spontaneously. By containing our own flow of ideas, rather than jumping in and interrupting as soon as we get them, we build interest and an excitement which characterizes genuine dialogue. For this reason, silence in the form of active listening is an energizing technique. It breeds good will and appreciation and stimulates a genuine exchange of ideas.

When we truly listen to another person, we honor them. The quality of our attention is the space we provide for another to be present with us. Taking other people that seriously can even be a form of spiritual practice, reminiscent of the Eastern practice of treating every guest as a manifestation of God who is gracing us by his or her visit.

This is a lot to say about silence. But of course it's not just silence. It's making room for another person, inviting him or her to come forth clearly and comfortably, honoring their process and our relationship at the same time. It's a skill that takes practice. It develops by degrees but benefits all concerned. We learn to consciously withhold judgments and assumptions, to restrain our habit of interrupting to re-focus attention on ourselves, and to give quality attention. By doing so, we create the safety for our partner to do the same.

LISTEN

When I ask you to listen to me

and you start giving me advice,

you have not done what I asked.

When I ask you to listen to me

and you begin to tell me why

I shouldn't feel that way,

you are trampling on my feelings.

When I ask you to listen to me

and you feel you have to do

something to solve my problem,

you have failed me, strange as that may seem.

Listen! All I asked was that you listen, not talk or do.

Just hear me.

Advice is cheap: twenty-five cents

will get you both Dear Abby and Billy Graham

in the same newspaper.

I can do that for myself; I'm not helpless;

maybe discouraged and faltering, but not helpless.

But when you accept as a simple fact

that I do feel what I feel,

no matter how irrational,

then I can quit trying to convince you

and can get about the business of understanding

what's behind this irrational feeling.

When that's clear, the answers are obvious

and I don't need advice.

Irrational feelings make sense

when we understand what's behind them.

Perhaps that's why prayer works, sometimes,

for some people –

because God is mute and doesn't give advice

or try to fix things.

He/She/It just listens and lets you work it out for yourself.

So please listen and just hear me.

And if you want to talk, wait a minute for your turn –

and I'll listen to you.

~ Anonymous

LISTENING EXERCISES

Silence in conversations feels awkward to some people. In writing, reflect on how it makes you feel, first with people you know well, then with people you don't know very well.

1. Ask yourself why you think you respond as you do to silence under different conditions? What role does anxiety play in your responses to these varying situations?

2. Relate one or two positive experiences you've had with silence, either alone or with others.

3. If you've never tried this, spend some hours or even half or a full day being utterly silent, alone or with others who agree to the same procedure. Don't participate in verbal communication of any kind. If you take a full day, include a meal and some outdoor activity like a walk or hike.

4. Note down any experiences you've had when judging others clouded your perception, resulting in a lost opportunity and /or embarrassment.

5. In the Active Listening exercise that follows, you'll need a partner. You, as a listener, have a responsibility to not jump in but to let your partner as speaker have as much time as s/he needs.

If in doubt as to whether the speaker is really finished, ask in a friendly way, "Are you finished?"

ACTIVE LISTENING EXERCISE

Here are complete guidelines for practicing active listening.

a. The speaker gets three minutes. The listener is the timekeeper.

b. The listener should give occasional feedback by

(1) encouraging

(2) asking for clarification and

(3) restating what you just heard.

c. When the speaker is finished, you, as listener, will summarize what your partner said, including how you think he or she feels about the topic.

d. The speaker will then give you feedback by telling you if you heard correctly and understood his/her feelings accurately. If not, the speaker will correct you. You should then repeat what s/he just told you so s/he knows for sure you understood. After completing this, switch roles.

Here are some topics to use, or use your own:

1. Are there any valid reasons for keeping secrets from (a) people you work with and (b) people you live with?

2. Talk about the most recent joyous occasion or upsetting incident you remember. After you've both finished, discuss the following with each other:

a. How did it feel to be attentively listened to by your partner?

b. If, as a listener, it was difficult to actively listen, say what was difficult about it.

THE CENTERING EXERCISE

There are many kinds of silence, each with its own purpose and impact. This exercise uses silence to reveal the influence of another person's psycho-physical presence on our ability to stay centered and focused.

Everyone has a personal space into which only close friends and intimates are welcomed. When someone else enters that space uninvited, either physically or energetically by virtue of their personality or by the power of their authority, we might get anxious and respond both physiologically and emotionally. Anxiety makes us breathe more rapidly and shallowly. We may start to sweat. We may even feel flustered, confused, or possibly defensive. In any case, what is often likely is that we will smile. This is an unbidden, inappropriate smile, because in this exercise (or in real life under such circumstances) there is really nothing to smile about. It is an anxiety smile. Most of the people I work with, when they experience it, deny that it's anxiety at first ("I'm just a smiley person," is a common response), but recognize it as the exercise continues, because with most people, it happens again and again until we get grounded. We should add that some people are well-grounded to begin with, or so comfortable with others that they may not respond with an "anxiety" smile. If you're one of them, try to recognize any internal sign of discomfort and use that as a signal of anxiety.

This exercise will give you the experience of monitoring and controlling anxiety as you identify and regulate the optimal psycho-physical distance between you and another person.

DIRECTIONS:

PART I.

1. Stand at opposite ends of the room and face each other. Close your eyes, relax your tummy and breathe quietly, from your belly, filling your lower lungs with air ("belly breathing"). Sense your body. Feel your feet pressing against the floor. Let your upper body weight drop into your belly, and bend your knees slightly, lowering your center of gravity. Try to get a feeling for yourself standing in this space. Be aware of your breath, your weight, your whole physical entity.

2. Check in with yourself emotionally to see how you're feeling at this moment. Notice and make note to yourself any feelings you have.

This active attention to your physical body and emotional state is what we call being grounded or centered. This state, where you are right now, is your base of operations. We'll call it "home base" or "being centered" and come back or refer back to it often. So settle in and be comfortable in this, your basic centered state.

3. Now drop your head a bit and open your eyes so you can see the floor. After a few seconds close your eyes again and return to home base. See if you lost any grounding when you opened your eyes.

4. Now, giving full attention to holding on to the feelings of home base, open your eyes again and look at the floor in front of you. Although you're looking at the floor, try not to allow your attention to go there. Keep your attention focused in your body instead. In other words, stay centered in home base while looking at the floor.

5. Once you can do that, raise your head and start looking slowly around the room without letting your attention flow out to any object you happen to see. Don't think about any of it. Keep your attention focused within yourself, physically and emotionally. If you lose home base, close your eyes for a moment until you get it back again.

PART II.

1. Breathe in the belly. Make brief eye contact with your partner. Hold eye contact for a few seconds, then drop your gaze to the floor again. Note to yourself if anything changed when you made eye contact.

Think about what happened when you made eye contact. You probably lost home base to some degree. Your attention probably flew to your partner instead of remaining focused within you. You may have lost your awareness of how you feel and started to think about how your partner feels about you, or even something completely unrelated.

Maybe you didn't, but most people tend to lose their center when they make eye contact with someone. If you lost your center, close your eyes for a moment until you get it back.

2. Make eye contact again, holding it for a few seconds longer.

3. Come back to home base by gazing at something neutral like the floor, or by closing your eyes. Now you're ready to see if you can make prolonged eye contact without losing your strong sense of self.

Look at your partner and hold eye contact. Use the belly breath to help you stay centered. Your partner's role is purely supportive, to be as fully present for you as possible. You'll do the same for him or her later. If you lose your center, just look away, down, or close your eyes, but as soon as you re-center yourself, go back to eye contact. You'll probably go in and out of center, in and out of eye contact for a bit, but the goal is to hold silent eye contact for about two minutes in a comfortable way without losing home base.

PART III.

As before, these instructions are for the person who will go first. Any time during this exercise that you lose center, stop, relax your tummy and breathe in the belly, look down or close your eyes until you get it back. Then continue, as follows:

1. As you hold silent eye contact and stay centered at the same time, walk very slowly towards your partner, one step at a time, while s/he stands still and holds eye contact with you. Take your time, move slowly, stop whenever you lose touch with home base, then start again.

Your partner is your ally. S/he should be open and supportive of what you're trying to do.

2. Come as close as you can to your partner without losing touch with home base. Don't smile or give any energy to him or her. If you smile, you can safely assume it's an anxiety smile and that you've lost your center, if even just a bit. Break eye contact, relax, breathe in the belly, then once re-centered, continue on. Keep your attention on your feelings and sensations.

3. At some point you will either enter your partner's personal space and feel uncomfortable about being "too close" (particularly if you are doing this exercise with someone you don't know well), or you will reach a point, beyond which you find you cannot come any closer without feeling anxious and losing your center..

If your partner feels you've come uncomfortably close, s/he may tell you to stop. This is important. If this happens, stop when s/he asks you to. And here's something for the partners: please note *your* reactions as this person comes closer and closer to you, especially if s/he comes *too* close for comfort.

4. To complete this part of the exercise, break eye contact and return to your side of the room, get centered in home base, then make eye contact with your partner again. Now it's your partner's turn to do what you just did. Feel free to talk with your partner about your experience.

Re-read directions so your partner can do it.

The awareness awakened by the centering exercise uses pro-active silence. In fact, the silence will be charged either by our anxiety, or by how much focused, centered attention we bring to it.

STEP 4. STAYING PRESENT

The level of presence, or mindfulness, we bring to our everyday dealings with people determines the degree of connection everyone will feel. If we're physically present but mentally and/or emotionally somewhere else, we won't feel very connected.

Few of us are trained in being fully present. We do it, but mostly unintentionally, as when we're absorbed in a good movie, play, piece of music or book. If asked what kind of mental muscle we used to attend with such absorption for so long a time, most of us wouldn't know how to answer.

Being fully present with someone is as much a discipline as going to the gym every day to work out, as much a commitment as sitting down to practice the piano regularly, or do a daily meditation.

> Inevitably, as our mind wanders ... we often see how little inner discipline, patience, or compassion we actually have. It doesn't take much time ... to see how scattered and unsteady our attention remains even when we try to direct and focus it ... Repeating our meditation, we relax and sink into the moment, deeply connecting with what is present ... We train ourselves to come back to this moment. What we need is a cup of understanding, a barrel of love, and an ocean of patience [74]

When we're fully present, we can love with freshness and innocence. If we're in a committed relationship, staying present keeps love as sparklingly alive as the day of its first bloom.

Occasionally that special feeling goes away. This usually occurs when our past conditioning gets in the way. It can happen just when we have the impression everything is on track. For example, just when we think we've finally resolved our issues with our parents, along comes a new upheaval of old experiences and we have to dismantle another piece of conditioning.

The past can intrude in relationships subtly. Bits of it can hide in the background or shadows of our relationship. Only discernment can bring them to light. They can be as subtle as tones of voice which reflect attitudes our parents showed toward us when we were young. They can be as obvious as the running conversations inside our heads that tell us we're good, bad or ugly.

Intrusions from the past are further obscured by the fact that when we're "in the past," we're generally unaware of it, like the fish that doesn't know it's wet.[75] It usually takes a partner or someone else to point out we're not fully present. Once we are present, we can look back and recognize the trance we've just come out of, like waking up from a dream. We can then reconstruct what just happened and identify characteristics of the old behavior.

For example, let's say someone identified a pattern, that when she is "in the past," one of the things she does, which she wouldn't normally do, is to get inappropriately angry if she feels someone she cares about is trying to put her down. She notices that she reacts defensively, raises her voice, and asserts in no uncertain terms what she won't put up with. To stay with this example, let's say her partner acknowledges his feelings, yes, it was a put-down, even apologizes, but comments that she's so angry he wonders if there isn't something else going on. Taking a cue from his comment and the intensity of her own reaction, she realizes some old program is running. This helps her notice the reaction in real time, so she is able to stop herself. She can then take a moment to reflect and ask herself, "What's going on?" That breaks the trance. In this case, she understands that she's responding to the put-down as though her partner was her father. She also realizes that she doesn't need to raise her voice for him to hear her. She realizes that she can describe what she thinks is going on and what she imagines her partner's role is. Then together they can get to the bottom of it.

This is an empowering moment and there is no end to the opportunities we all have to experience something like this. For example, I remember when my significant other told me I didn't know how to work the tape recorder correctly. This was an audio dubbing deck I'd purchased a few years ago and was very familiar with. I was preparing a musical collage, and the dubbing had to be precise. It was a trick I wanted to master. I was completely absorbed in the process and thrilled about my discovery that these pieces of classical music from three different centuries fit together beautifully. But when he came over and said, "Let me help" and started telling me how to do it, I automatically deferred. After all, he was the classical music expert and had been recording dozens of selections since I'd known him. And I had unconscious lingerings of my old conditioning that boys knew more about electronics than girls.

My partner gave subtle clues that he felt superior, so subtle I didn't notice them. But I started feeling more and more frustrated and finally angry, not knowing why. While we were in the midst of this, a friend stopped by. She noticed my partner was acting condescending toward me, and she said so. This made me feel less crazy for feeling angry. I got up the nerve to tell him he was patronizing me, but I couldn't put my finger on how. He didn't get it. He denied having an attitude or tone of voice. But I felt so strongly he was doing *something*, I couldn't let go of it.

It took weeks and a few more similar occurrences for us identify what was going on. I finally realized he couldn't see in himself what I experienced frequently. We finally understood that he went into his unconscious fallback position under stress, which was to take control and feel superior. This pressured me to take a one-down position, which I hated. I'd had that up to my eyeballs growing up with a patronizing father. I reacted so angrily to my partner's attitude that he had to defend himself even more.

We couldn't break the cycle, however, without identifying my own part in overreacting, and his part in treating me, as it turned out, the way his father had treated him. My partner put me in the position his father had put him in. As a child, my partner had been put down so often he'd come to feel it was normal. This was what made it so hard for him to understand my upset at being patronized.

Once we saw the pattern, we could stay conscious of it, and for the most part stop the old behaviors.

We didn't completely rid ourselves of this particular shadow from the past, however. In fact, both our fathers lurked around, showing up now and then, as unconscious influences. When this happened, we both felt something was wrong, but it takes detective work to figure out exactly what's going on. We're no longer surprised to find the subtle influence of parents and in-laws interfering in our lives and those of our clients.

In real life, our parents and in-laws don't generally interfere. And they're nice enough people. What interferes are our internal characterizations of them we learned in childhood, when we were impressionable and they were inexperienced in being parents. For more discussion about unexpected intrusions of old trauma, see the discussion of Testing in Step 3, earlier in this chapter.

TIME TRAVELING

We need to make a daily practice of staying present. This means paying attention to what we think and where our focus wanders throughout the course of each day. We can lose presence by worrying "what if," by wondering how our future will turn out, by dwelling on the past out of self pity or for any other reason, by pointing the finger at others, by passing the buck in hundreds of tiny ways. All these daily ways we lose presence we call Time Traveling, because our mind wanders to another time and place.

Meditation teachers such as Jack Kornfield have described the persistence required to cultivate presence and bring ourselves back when we've gone elsewhere:

> For some, this task of coming back a thousand or ten thousand times in meditation may seem boring or even of questionable importance. But how many times have we gone away from the reality of our life? – perhaps a

million or ten million times! If we wish to awaken, we have to find our way back here with our full being, our full attention ... Bring yourself back to the point quite gently. And even if you do nothing during the whole of your hour but bring your heart back a thousand times, though it went away every time you brought it back, your hour would be very well employed.[76]

While this commentary refers to the practice of meditation, it's aptly compared to staying present in our relationships. We need during the course of our time with others to refocus our attention again and again on the person to whom we are listening. This is no easy task, for we are challenging the nature of mind itself in its drive to ever seek the new.

When we're with another person, Time Traveling robs us of our shared intimacy. We may not even be aware of not being fully present until we come back from our reveries with a start and realize we'd tuned out. Some people are so used to not being present they think it's normal and wonder why their partner loses interest and their relationship goes stale.

Ways to repair relationship damage caused by not being present are simple but require humility. The most basic is to confess that we tuned out and haven't heard what was just said. This works with friends, intimate partners and even in work situations. It's better to admit one's mistake and get the information repeated than to pretend we heard. Next we need to identify the emotional trigger which took us out of the present. Which direction did we travel? What was the content, mood or feeling of our fantasy?

The more self aware we become, the more easily we catch ourselves drifting and can bring ourselves back.

EXERCISES FOR STAYING PRESENT

1. RHYTHM

The goal of this exercise is to establish, maintain and then vary specific rhythm patterns, using your hands. At least two people are needed. A larger group makes these exercises more challenging and fun.

> The pattern is in waltz time. Using three beats, clap your hands twice, then snap your fingers once: CLAP - CLAP - SNAP. One set of three movements should merge with the next to produce a continuously rhythmic sound. Try it a few times just to get the feel and sound of it.

> Now increase the speed of the rhythm. This requires attention. The pattern can't be maintained unless each person stays alert. One person should volunteer to lead a gradual increase in speed.

> The third part of this exercise is especially challenging in a large group. It requires a surprising amount of attention. Only one person at a time will clap - clap - snap. Decide who will go first and determine what the order or direction will be. Then try it at different speeds and see how fast you can go and maintain a smooth flow.

When a group is operating with a high level of attention, as is necessary to accomplish a task like this, it generates excitement. The task itself fades into the background. Presence is what counts. The task could be a game of basketball among friends, an important discussion between lovers, or high level negotiations with international consequences. If everyone is fully involved, a flow state is achieved which carries people along in a supra-natural state of energy and coordination. The feeling is expansive and exhilarating. We experience a satisfying sense of mastery independent of the actual outcome.

2. INSIGHT MEDITATION

Insight or Vipassana meditation develops our mental muscle used in staying present. You may have heard the prescription for achieving enlightenment by chopping wood and carrying water. This is a metaphor for full participation and awareness of what is. The heart of Insight Meditation is keeping an exclusive focus in the present by, for example, connecting our attention to our breathing.

The heart of Insight Meditation is keeping an exclusive focus in the present by, for example, connecting our attention to our breathing.

Focusing on the breath is just one form of mindfulness. We could concentrate on virtually anything. But to maintain our concentration also requires alertness to keep us focused there. Otherwise we may fall asleep or get distracted.

The breath (or whatever we are focusing on) and our alertness work together, training the mind to stay in one place. With practice we wander less and less, as we strengthen control over our own mental process.

Jack Kornfield says that learning how to meditate is similar to training a puppy. You put the puppy down and say, "Stay." Does the puppy listen? It gets up and it runs away. You sit the puppy back down again. "Stay." And the puppy runs away over and over again. Sometimes the puppy jumps up, runs over, and pees in the corner or makes some other mess. Our minds are much the same as the puppy, only they create even bigger messes. In training the mind, or the puppy, we have to start over and over again...but always remember that in training a puppy we want to end up with the puppy as our friend.[77]

3. THE 80/20 RULE

The 80/20 rule is an application of the meditative frame of mind while in the midst of daily activity. It means keeping 80% of our attention on the subject at hand, while at the same time keeping the other 20% in the world of sensation, of our breath, or how it *feels* to sit or stand where we are, or where our hands are resting, and so on. Although we can't think of two things at the same time, we can think and feel at the same time. The split focus helps keep us grounded in the present moment.

4. ALPHACENTRICS™ BREATHING METHOD

One of the most effective methods for clearing the mind of distractions and becom-ing present is a breath technique we teach called AlphaCentrics. It's effective because it works at the root of the problem, which is anxiety plus accumulated life stress. To practice AlphaCentrics, lie on your back, eyes closed, and and inhale smoothly, through the nose, until you have taken a full breath, filling up your belly all the way. Then exhale through the nose, flattening your belly all the way down. Don't let your breath go up into the chest. (For most people, this takes practice.) Repeat this, in a one-two-three rhythm, like waltz-time – three counts to inhale, three counts to exhale. Continue this for twenty to forty minutes at a time. You will have to relax your tummy muscles to keep your breath down low and not let it go up into the chest.

Abdominal breathing stimulates the relaxation response and takes us quickly into a meditative, or alpha state, enabling the body to heal and recuperate, physically, emotionally, and spiritually. You can do this on your own without risk, but if you have any trouble, can't get out of chest breathing, or want to learn more advanced AlphaCentrics techniques, which require supervision, please contact the authors.

STEP 5. TAKE EMOTIONAL RISKS

TELLING THE TRUTH

Our work with couples has convinced us that, contrary to popular belief, good relationships take work and are not automatically self-sustaining. We've seen the truth of the saying, "a relationship is only as sick as its secrets." It's better to err on the side of disclosure than withholding. For psychological health, couples need to tell each other even the microscopic truth. It's a skill set well worth learning and practicing. The microscopic truth includes the ongoing subtle variations in who we are, our ever-changing combination of moods and feelings. Disclosing our inner experience brings interest, color and appeal to our relationships.

Being over forty and having lived in the San Francisco Bay Area most of my life, I have vivid memories of the "light shows" put on at the Fillmore and Avalon Ballroom in the late sixties. The screens on which these brilliant, pulsing displays were projected formed a border, but within these frames there was a constantly changing flow of color, form and mood. So it is with the myriad changes in our thoughts, moods, and feelings.

TURN UP THE VOLUME

We may not believe that someone we have our eye on could genuinely be interested in all of our changes. We may never have gotten that message from busy, distracted or emotionally unavailable parents.

We tell most couples – and frankly, it's usually the men who have the most trouble with this – to "turn up the volume," that is, to share more of their internal life with their partners. "S/he wants to know more. Share your ideas, express your feelings, check out your assumptions, clear lingering resentments, even little ones," we tell them. This kind of sharing is the hallmark of authenticity and the foundation stone of genuine intimacy.

But it feels risky. We might be judged, rejected, ridiculed, humiliated or criticized. Fear of vulnerability is common, for these reasons. For most of us, our whole lives discouraged being open. Had we been taught growing up how to defend ourselves by means other than closing down or getting angry, we'd be more willing to open ourselves.

CHECKING IT OUT

To clear the way to take emotional risks, we need to examine our expectations of what we imagine will happen if we do. The first expectation is usually the belief that people want to make us wrong or contradict what we think is in our best interest. With some exceptions, this is not true. Most people welcome openness in others and respond in a less defended way once we open the door.

For example, one client related how he went through hell five times before finally getting up enough courage to come out to his family as a proud gay man. He didn't know what would happen but expected the worst. His older brother, with whom he was not close, did react badly and hasn't spoken to him since. However, much to his surprise, his parents were actually relieved by his revelation. They had known at some level for a long time that he was gay but didn't want to confirm their suspicions.

After an initial difficult adjustment, they accepted his sexual preference and its accompanying lifestyle, giving him space and permission to share his life with them.

Our willingness to take risks changes when two things are in place: (1) we expect good treatment, and (2) we know how to stand up for ourselves if we're treated otherwise.

If we're afraid, we invite attack in response to our expectation of bad things happening. People do this on an unconscious level, so we need to be sure we're not letting unconscious expectations spoil things for us.

While being real can be risky, not coming forward runs an even greater risk. We've all seen too many empty relationships that have lasted too long, either because of convenience, for the sake of the children, or because neither partner could tell the truth. And relationships that have wonderful potential can be rendered sterile by emotional withholding. But because of the paucity of historical precedent in our lives for authentic behavior, we can't assess whether the danger of coming forth is real or imaginary. The only way to find out is to take a risk and check it out by saying what we truly think and feel or what awful thing we're imagining. We'll usually discover the danger has been only imagined.

The kinds of emotional risk-taking most feared usually have to do with confronting family secrets or taboos, such as alcoholism.

Keeping quiet prolongs the agony or dysfunction, but speaking up seems to portend dire consequences. Speaking up would be easier if someone had shown us how to do it. We described in Step 2 a neutral way to say virtually anything, and this formula works for nearly every communication dysfunction except those involving addiction or severe psychological dysfunction.

Taking emotional risks increases our freedom by widening our range of choice. We give ourselves more options than to be defensive, angry or withholding when we feel upset by something.

It's important to take the risk and talk about something that's bothering us, even if it seems so small, so petty, that we think it couldn't be worth the effort, as the following story illustrates:

> When I first started dating Lauren, I noticed she had a short neck. After a while this started to bother me. I kept quiet about it because after all, what could she do about it, assuming she would even want to? I told myself this was one of those non-negotiables. There's nothing to say. You either accept it or you don't.
>
> I had trouble with this and started to pull away. She quickly picked up on my feelings and knew something was wrong but couldn't have known what it was. So she asked me point blank, and I had to decide what to do. If I withheld, I might save some face, but the way things were going it might spell the end of our relationship.
>
> I decided I liked her enough to risk telling the truth, so looking her straight in the eye, I said, "I know this sounds stupid, but I think you have a short neck and it really bothers me" and waited for the axe to fall.
>
> Her surprised silence only lasted a second. Despite my fantasies about how she might react, I was totally unprepared for what happened.
>
> She laughed! With a mixture of amusement, relief and without any hint of pain, contempt or anger, she said, "People have told me that. I'm so glad that's all it is. I thought you were getting cold feet! By the way, I'm also long-waisted. Does that bother you too?"

Tears sprang to my eyes as resentment and pent up feelings of frustration and confusion melted away. In that moment of honesty and connection I realized that my feelings had really been about fear of growing intimacy. I reaffirmed my desire to stay with her. By her laughter and response she taught me some important lessons: that it was safe to talk about whatever bothers me; that she accepted herself as she was and if I didn't like it, it was my problem, not hers; and most importantly that, by implication, I didn't have to be perfect either for her to care about me. All I had to be was myself. We got married a year later.

What a paradox! How is it that out of seemingly rejecting statements come relief and greater intimacy?

Such statements only appear to be rejecting. They are actually ways of saying "no" to the fear of being swallowed up or treated badly in the name of love. They're limit-setters, boundary markers, and they help define a person as being a clearly separate entity. How can we love someone if we don't know who they are? People fumble and struggle with this issue of being separate, standing up for themselves and getting their own needs met, fearing that if we aren't the same then we can't stay together. But the opposite is more often true. There are very few people who would be interested in being married to a mirror image of themselves. Although common ground is important, diversity and uniqueness bring spice and growth to a relationship that would not be there without it.

It's the strong sense of self and its clear expression that is the basis for being seen, appreciated and truly loved. The real building of intimacy starts after the haze of romance has burned off and two unique individuals stand fearlessly face-to-face. Then you can see each other clearly as separate and distinct individuals who want to work something out together.

EXERCISES

1. Name some issues which qualify as emotionally risky for you to talk about, (a) growing up in your family, (b) in your current family or circle of friends, (c) at work.

2. Describe any role model you've had for taking emotional risks in a healthy way. How has that example touched you?

3. Whom do you know and interact with who gives you support to take emotional risks?

4. What is it about this person or these people that makes it safe to be yourself around them?

5. Whom do you know and interact with (or have stopped interacting with) because it didn't feel safe to take emotional risks with them?

6. Why is it unsafe with this person or these people?

7. How do you deal with your feelings around these people?

8. Think of one or more current situations in which taking an emotional risk to clear the air with someone is both needed

and possible. Write down the name(s), then take a moment to close your eyes and do the following visualization: See your-self taking risks and being received in an open, positive way by this person.

9. Decide with whom on this list you will actually complete your un-finished business. Hopefully you can meet with them all eventually. Write down for each person their name, the date by which you hope to do this, and your plan of action (yes, you should develop one). After each meeting, note down your thoughts and feelings about what happened.

STEP 6. LETTING GO

In the end, just three things matter:

How well we have lived,
How well we have loved,
How well we have learned to let go.
~ *Buddhist saying*

There's a story about a man climbing the side of a cliff, who reached an impasse. Not able to go up or down, he panicked, lost his footing and started to fall. Catching a tree root which stuck out of the rock, he hung, suspended, forty feet off the ground. Gazing up he desperately cried out, "If there's anybody up there, please save me!" Within seconds came a thunderous voice from the clouds, "My son, I hear you, and I will save you, but first you must let go of the branch." The man thought about it for a second, looked down, looked back up, and shouted, "Is there anybody else up there?"

Assistance for the rock climber was dependent on his letting go of the branch, which was precisely what he could not bring himself to do. The fear of falling and his conditioned reflex to hold on was too strong. And who would blame him? He saw the branch as a lifeline, but it was illusory. We all have at least a few of these illusory lifelines that we're hanging on to.

This classic irony is played out time and again with old patterns of belief and behavior which once had survival value but which are now dysfunctional or self-destructive. Claire's case is an example, Claire quickly got sexual with the men she was dating, and discovered afterwards that her partner was wrong for her. She said, "I feel so empty when I'm alone, it seems I need a man to fill me up. And if I don't relate to a man sexually, I don't know how to act."

The beliefs Claire was held to by this particular illusory lifeline was that she could not have the intimacy she longed for except by being sexual, and that she wouldn't be accepted if she acted according to the non-sexual feelings she might have.

Claire believed she had to play the seductress to get her needs met. The rock climber believed he would fall and die. In both instances the larger issue, transferable to many conditions and circumstances, is that of giving up control and power. As we saw earlier, power/control is one of the three basic hidden agendas most everyone has. Autonomy is a major developmental milestone and vitally important to our happiness and well-being as an adult. We are helpless for so long as infants that the gradually unfolding acquisition of independence is like a miracle. Autonomy, for those so fortunate as to have achieved it, is a hard-fought victory and we are loathe to give it up.

The struggle for independence doesn't end with adolescence. We may be on our own, but still trying to fit square pegs into round holes, hoping to mold others to our sense of how they should be, struggling to alter circumstances and conditions to suit our needs rather than accepting reality as it is.

Ask the partner of an alcoholic or addict what it's like trying to live with a user and not be codependent, that is, not trying to control the user, the use, and its consequences. Despite the fact that trying to save someone from the consequences of any self-destructive behavior is a noble endeavor, attempting to accomplish this by executive command, threats, cajoling, enabling, or any other external means is virtually impossible without physically locking someone up.

Research by AA (Alcoholics Anonymous) and other Twelve-Step groups supports the contention that trying to control someone else's behavior is not only an illusion, but a potentially lethal one at that. Despite their passionate advocacy of, and plea for, sanity by letting go of it, this illusion is highly prized and morbidly persistent.[78]

If the ability to control things is an illusion, how should we live in an imperfect world? Should we not be pro-active and seek positive changes for ourselves and others? To be sure, yes, we should try and never stop trying. There is always something, even a small change, that can make a difference. But social and political activism is different from trying to "fix" someone's attitude or change their behavior (if they are not on board) to get things the way we think they ought to be. The constant attempts to force those changes confuse and wreak havoc with relationships.

What? You don't love me anymore?
What? You're walking out the door?
What? You don't like the way I chew?
Hey, let me tell you.
You're not the woman that I wed.
You say you're depressed but you're not.
You just like to stay in bed.
I don't need you, darling Lorraine.
Darling Lorraine...
Lorraine
I long for your love...

(Paul Simon, "Darling Lorraine")

The desire for control is so compelling that it prevents our becoming aware of its essentially illusory nature, so the question remains, over what do we actually have control? Like fish that swim in water but are unaware they're wet, oblivious to water's nature and influence, so are we motivated, often unconsciously, by attitudes and values shaped by our environment and past experience. And when we include unconscious factors, especially around mate selection, the degree of decision-making that is influenced by these unconscious factors is surprisingly great.

It's difficult even to control our own thoughts, as I'm sure you've realized if you've tried to meditate or deliberately not think about something specific. In the realm of personal relationships, the only thing we really have control over is how we react to our experiences. In the arena of response, we are truly in the driver's seat. Most everything else is outside our ability to affect the outcome, despite sensible efforts we all make to try and improve our lives.

Detachment is the key to letting go. If we properly understand detachment, we can recognize our limits and let go of what we can't control, which is the lion's share of most everything we try to do. Detachment does not mean giving up our efforts to achieve, accomplish, and improve our lives and the world in general.

Faced with this built-in contradiction – that our nature compels us to try to influence people and situations that are far too complex for us to change – exactly what is it that we should "let go" of? The answer is that, while we do our best to bring about outcomes we want, we can let go of the need to control how things turn out. In other words, detachment means giving up the need to control outcomes and detachment is the key to letting go.

Although we might be worried that letting go might harm our self-esteem, it won't, because who we are is not connected with outcomes. Self-esteem is connected to how authentic we can be in the process that leads to outcomes. We can set goals, choose means, act with integrity, and learn to accept what happens to us with equanimity, all without damage to our self-esteem, even if the outcome isn't all we hoped for. Detachment allows us to see reality as it is and accept it on its own terms.

Service and activism are sacrificial in that sense, but they are also self-reinforcing. It feels good to take a step, to help someone out – even a failed attempt feels good. It enables us to accurately perceive our limits and give up the illusion of control. It is an attitudinal change we do have control over, a skill to be practiced and mastered. We can envision the possible and work toward lofty goals. We can map out the territory and set out to become the person we want to be. That is why people everywhere keep making sparks even in the darkest dungeons. This allows the flame of hope to live and burn brightly, otherwise it, and we, would surely burn out.

By letting go, we can drop judgment, blame, criticism, unreasonable demand, and the tendency to make unwarranted assumptions. Yet this is no easy task. There may be many things we know we should let go of, but it's unlikely anyone could just make a list and check things off. Strange as it seems, we have to be ready to lay these burdens down. Just knowing about it isn't enough.

As an old story goes, there was an old man sitting on his porch with his dog and the dog was moaning. "Why is your dog moaning," asked a neighbor. The old man replied, "Oh, he's just sittin' on a nail." "Well, why doesn't he get up?" asked the neighbor. The man replied "Doesn't hurt enough yet."

Readiness comes from a private inner place and there's no telling how much pain a person can tolerate. There are many reasons why we've been holding on to our burdens. We can't discount that. And even if we clearly see how hurtful and dysfunctional it is to keep holding on to something, we can still be kind to ourselves if we aren't quite ready to get up off that nail just yet. Let's honor resistance. It's there for good reason. If we don't work through all that before trying to drop it, it's not going to work and we're likely to beat ourselves up for yet another example of how we're not good enough. It's a trap to try to force it. But if we stay aware, be mindful, hold the intention, at some point we will manage it. By letting go we further open ourselves to the excitement and joy of living authentically, bringing us closer to emotional freedom, peace of mind and the last step in this process, the power to forgive.

EXERCISE IN LETTING GO

Take a moment to sit quietly and calmly. Relax your tummy and breathe easily from the lower lung, allowing the belly to move gently out when you inhale, and back in when you exhale. Stay aware of your breathing and try to keep it in the "belly" as you do this exercise.

Visualize something (or someone) you need to let go of.

Now imagine you're standing before a symbol of the perfect union of spirit and matter, fire, perhaps an image of a magnificent bonfire on the beach at night.

The flames are burning brightly. You can hear the wood crackling, see the sparks flying, and feel the intense heat. Yet you know instinctively that you cannot be burned by this fire, even though you are standing close to it.

Take any lingering feelings about this situation or person, anger, bitterness, hurt, unhealed wounds or whatever there is, and picture these as pinecones on the ground at your feet. Imagine yourself picking them up and throwing them into the fire, watching them start to glow and finally burst into brilliant flame, until they are completely consumed.

STEP 7. FORGIVENESS

The path of authenticity is an uphill climb. Regrets for past mistakes, toward ourselves and others, and the pain of injustices done to us through the years but especially when we were young, weigh us down with guilt, anger, sadness, and other burdensome feelings. The task is not to stop feeling, but to somehow work through these difficult emotions, let them go, and in this final step, nurture forgiveness for ourselves, and others, for our own and for their transgressions. Without forgiveness, and especially self-forgiveness, we can't thoroughly relieve the pain or absolve the guilt.

Forgiveness is eloquently defined by psychologist Robert Enright, professor of educational psychology at the University of Wisconsin, Madison:

> "[Forgiveness is] a willingness to abandon one's right to resentment, negative judgment, and indifferent behavior toward one who unjustly hurt us, while fostering the undeserved qualities of compassion, generosity and even love toward him or her."[79]

That which lies unforgiven within us is like emotional inflammation. It causes pain and suffering. It barricades our heart from being fully open, through self-righteousness, resentment, defensiveness, or just plain embarrassment.

Cultivating forgiveness is an ancient tradition. Its power is reflected everywhere, in all the world's religions, as part of our celebration of important holidays, and as part of the guidance we offer to our children and grandchildren as they grow. We also find it in healing traditions like Twelve-Step, which have helped millions of people work through addiction, at least partially by laying down the burdens of guilt and anger over past wrongs, done and received.

Injustice to children is common, but usually unintentional, the product of poor parenting skills or a lack of education and common sense. Although most parents don't consciously or maliciously burden their children with their own pain or neediness, the number of families in this country where this process is alive and well is staggering, with some estimates as high as 90%.[80]

As we saw earlier (in Chapter 2), moved by a parent's neediness or pain, children try to help in any way possible, even at their own expense, and children who give up their own feelings and, in many cases, most of their childhoods, in order to emotionally shore up a needy parent, generally develop low self-esteem.

For example, when an authoritarian father puffs himself up to cover his feelings of inadequacy, his child may make sense of this by forming an unconscious belief that he can help his father by acting small and incompetent. When an overwhelmed mother withdraws and isolates herself in a world of anxiety and loneliness, her child may come to believe she can help by also becoming anxious and isolated, thus sharing the burden.

Those unfair pressures take their toll, and our poignant efforts never measure up. How could they? Yet even today we're hard on ourselves for somehow not being "good enough." And adults who, as children, developed habits of self-diminishment and self-sacrifice, will inevitably run into problems both in love and at work.

Because of the powerful body-mind connection, this can have disastrous consequences. As one woman put it:

> All the years of beating myself up, feeling I simply did not fit in this world, and expecting only the worst, [my expectations] turned on me and gave me cancer.[81]

Instead of continuing to beat ourselves up, we can address our shortcomings for what they are, the attempts of children to make sense out of incomprehensible and traumatic circumstances, fueled by innate altruism towards those they love and depend on. Children have been shown to manifest such generous and self-sacrificial behavior as early as 18 months.[82]

This awareness should make it easier, at least on a conscious level, for us to not only forgive those who harmed us, but also to ease up and forgive ourselves for these "imaginary crimes,"[83] by which we inhibited ourselves in order to help a parent or sibling. We may have been punishing ourselves for years for normal developmental steps that felt like crimes because we worried our parents would feel hurt by our growing up, or for doing things the way we best knew how, without the help and support children need and deserve.[84]

We can forgive ourselves for mistakes generated out of our intrinsic desire to be loving and caring, for inhibiting ourselves in order to help a parent or sibling.

Given the intrinsic unfairness and impossibility of these tasks and their self-sacrificial nature, it's not hard to see how many of us may emerge from our formative years with a warped sense of relationship, low self-esteem, and an ingrained belief in our own incompetence, ineffectiveness, and essentially flawed nature. All of these beliefs are firmly anchored by guilt, and its overblown status in our conditioning and our cultural and religious traditions, make it one of the most formidable of all emotional obstacles.

Although guilt is important in the development and expression of a conscience, what we're concerned with here is inappropriate guilt and the need for self-punishment for imaginary crimes,

crimes against basic and natural hopes and strivings, such as becoming independent and successful, which we have discussed in some detail in Chapter 2.

Forgiveness is the last of the seven steps. Its fulfillment requires the skill and confidence developed by the previous six, but it supports and helps maintain them at the same time. By working with these steps and intentionally walking the path of personal authenticity, we can find, hold, and maintain a loving, caring relationship, with the possibility of being loved unconditionally for who we really are.

EXERCISES IN SELF FORGIVENESS

Meditation and Visualization #1

We can ask for, and extend, forgiveness by inculcating compassion for ourselves and others.

The word "compassion" comes from a Latin base meaning "to suffer with" or "to suffer together." As we develop compassion, we become more aware of the suffering of others and awaken a desire to alleviate it. This doesn't mean forgetting the past, or pretending those injuries we have received or given no longer matter.

To be more specific, we don't want to deny our feelings of being wronged or hurt. Nor do we want to ignore the possibility of being wronged or hurt again by the same (or a similarly hurtful) person. A habitually abusive person may be unable or unwilling to change or accept help, yet some people stay in or go back into bad or toxic relationships with such people, thinking they can forgive and forget, or be a positive influence. But trying to change another person's attitude or behavior when that person's not on board, is futile. We can't expect much in a situation like that.

So the injuries matter, but as we learned in Step 6, we can let go of certain things that once mattered a great deal but over which we have no control. That includes thoughts of getting or regrets over "should have," "would have," "could have." What matters more is the realization that we can buck the internal tide of our conditioned opinions, biases, and judgments about what happened and the role we or others played in it.

Compassion and empathy are closely related but are not exactly the same. Compassion requires an empathic response to someone else's situation, allowing us to inquire into and understand what another person is going through, where they're coming from, and maybe even why they hurt us. But compassion goes one step further, giving us inner distance from another's pain and suffering, preventing us from cnfusing their pain with our own. As it turns out, this is an essential form of detachment, because empahty without compassion can be disastrously stressful.

According to the latest research in neuroscience,[85] when we truly empathize with another's pain, this resonance stimulates areas of our brain's neural network for unpleasantness and aversion. For example, if my partner for whatever reason is in chronic emotional or physical pain and I am constantly empathic with him/ her, I am at risk for stress, burnout, and poor health. Without a compassionate response in addition to empathy, at the very least I will need to withdraw or find respite before I burn out. In my work supporting cancer patients, I have learned that caregiver burn-out (when a spouse, or even a child, is ill) claims many relationships without the safety valve provided by a compassionate as well as an empathic caregiver response.

Empathy with compassion and the resulting detachment enable us to be effective, or not, without our getting stressed or burned-out. And for ourselves and our own situations, we can do the same, becoming more accepting of ourselves as we emerge from old patterns of negativity and soften the voice of our inner critic.

Empathy and compassion together build a groundwork of understanding that promotes emotional safety, so we can reasonably work out a resolution. They also help us accept if there is no resolution or compatibility, so we could either let go of the issue, or, if necessary, leave the relationship. This dual approach does not blur our vision of the past nor sweep anything under the rug. It turns down the volume on our judgments, opens our heart and impels us to action, while allowing us to relinquish needing to control the outcome. And the bottom line is, compassion allows us to forgive.

Forgiveness is the last of the seven steps. Its fulfillment requires the skill and confidence developed by the previous six, but it supports and helps maintain them at the same time. By working with these steps and intentionally walking the path of personal authenticity, we can find, hold, and maintain a loving, caring relationship, with the possibility of being loved unconditionally for who we really are.

EXERCISES IN FORGIVENESS FOR SELF AND OTHERS

MEDITATION AND VISUALIZATION #1

One way to awaken compassion and indirectly address forgiveness would be to repeat to oneself, and think about, the simple phrases of the Buddhist meditation known as "Loving Kindness":

May I be filled with loving kindness.
May I be well in body and mind.
May I be safe from inner and outer dangers.
May I be truly happy and free.

As we work with these phrases, we can change the "I" to "you," starting with a loved one, then to specific friends or family, then moving out to others not so close to us, and eventually even to people we dislike or whom have actually hurt us. We can also change the "you" to "we," thinking of our family members and those near and dear to us, and then moving out to friends and neighbors, associates, others we meet, and eventually to all members of our human family.

We can do this while walking, sitting quietly, or even while driving instead of letting the mind wander, something we know we shouldn't do while driving but everybody does it. So we might as well put our thoughts somewhere constructive.

A more direct approach, when considering how we may have hurt others, would be to say to oneself something like this:

For any harm or pain I've caused,
knowingly or unknowingly,
I ask forgiveness.

Visualize a particular person while doing this, or do it in a more general way.

When it comes to self-forgiveness, just vary the first and last line:

For any harm or pain I've caused myself,
knowingly or unknowingly,
I forgive myself.

And to help us forgive those who have harmed us, we could say, while visualizing them:

For the harm and pain you've caused me,
knowingly or unknowingly,
I forgive you.

This forgiveness meditation, above, is based on teachings found on-line of Vipassana teacher Jack Kornfield.[85]

As effective as this practice is over time, it is decidedly not a quick fix. We may have harbored pain, guilt, regret, and various grudges for many years, sometimes all our lives. So we shouldn't expect that we can let them go easily, nor should we criticize or judge ourselves for that.

A friend of ours related his experience working with these techniques:

> I remember when I first tried this, I wanted to forgive my father for various childhood incidents. I was taking a walk on a pleasant morning. I began with the loving kindness meditation, then visualized him and started saying the lines about forgiveness. I literally got sick to my stomach and had to stop. I clearly wasn't ready and didn't try again for some time. At first I heard the jury in my head, chastising me for my failure, but I ignored it. I used the Loving Kindness meditation for myself, and then, changing the lines slightly I included him by saying "you" instead of "I," while visualizing him. This was also difficult, but eventually got easier. Maybe six months later I tried forgiving him again and this time made some progress.

Meditation and Visualization #2

You may want to have someone read these directions aloud to you.

1. Sit or lie comfortably in a place where you won't be interrupted. Close your eyes and take three or four deep breaths, breathing all the way down into your belly. Then continue breathing in your belly, preferably through the nose. Imagine yourself at age three or four. Perhaps you can see yourself in a room with furniture you recognize. You may even recognize clothing the little child is wearing. After watching for a moment, let the child know you're there, and make eye contact. The child knows who you are and is glad to see you. Go over to the child and sit on the floor together.

Open your arms to the child, who wants to be embraced by you. Tell the child how wonderful s/he is and how much you love him or her, that you understand exactly what s/he's going through, and that you forgive him or her for anything s/he feels guilty about. Let the child know that whatever's going on in the family is not his or her fault.

2. Now separate from the child. Tell him or her again how wonderful s/he is, how much you love him or her, and say goodbye. In your mind's eye, see yourself in the house where you lived when you were nine years old. Again, go to your room, look around and make contact with the nine-year-old you meet there, who is you at that age. Do with this child what you did with the three-year-old. When you've completed this, say goodbye and, in your mind's eye, go over to a window in the room. Outside it's a beautiful day and you see a teenager. It's you at about age sixteen, give or take a few years. Go outside and be with him or her. S/he knows who you are and is glad to see you. Do the same with this image of yourself as you did before, sending the message of love and forgiveness.

3. Do the same for yourself as a young adult of about twenty-six or so. If you're much over forty, do this up to about fifteen years of your current age.

4. Now come face to face with yourself as you are today, but see yourself all wrapped in bandages, like a mummy. These bandages are the bonds of limitation caused by guilt for all your imaginary crimes as well as mistakes you've actually made.

5. Now gently peel off the bandages from around your head, watching them fall from your eyes and ears, until you can clearly see your own face. Now cut the bandages away from your arms and chest and feel the expansiveness as you breathe easily again. Cut away the remaining bandages from your legs so you can once again move freely without the burden of unconscious guilt.

6. As you see yourself at last unencumbered and released, feel yourself surrounded by light, love and appreciation for who you are. Knowing what you now know about why you made some of your mistakes, absolve yourself of guilt. Tell yourself you're forgiven, that you don't have to act that way anymore, that there were other forces involved, that you'll no longer allow yourself to be victimized by other's neediness, that you no longer need to hold on to your anger, fear, pain or guilt, and that you're willing to let go of them, right now.

7. Note down what this felt like.

In certain cases, this visualization, powerful as it is, may not fully complete all the layers of your experience. These may surface at another time. Whenever new pieces of experience come to mind, you can repeat this exercise and visualization.

Conclusion

THE CRUCIBLE FOR CHANGE

Some people believe we need to change social institutions in order to change people; that social change leads to individual growth and development. Others believe we can change the quality of life and society more directly by working on ourselves, because society is made up of individuals.

We can strike a balance between inner and outer-directed efforts towards change. Relationship, be it through service or intimacy, is as important in its own way as internal personal work. Both free us to be open, to understand, relate and provide a testing ground for practicing authenticity.

There was a popular saying a while back, "Men should come with directions." Everyone got a laugh out of this. We think the need for directions applies to *all* romantic relationships, and even to life itself. How strange that we should need a guidebook to remind us to be who we really are. Yet that's the way it is today.

We've tried to give structure to the process of moving ahead on the path of authenticity, self-awareness and human connection. This path is no longer "the road less travelled" as M. Scott Peck suggested.[86] We're all being influenced, consciously or unconsciously by a profound cultural paradigm shift which has occurred over the past decades. The shift is reaching into our work lives, our social lives and our intimate relationships. Some believe it represents a quantum leap in the evolution of humanity.

> People inside and outside the corporation are more self-reliant and empowered, to be sure; they have also shifted their value emphasis. Economic and status values (position, display of wealth) carry less weight; quality-of-life related values: self-realization, spiritual discovery, quality of relationships, quality of the environment, fairness of the system, well-being of future generations, concern for the long-term viability of the global system – all these show up in surveys and other data to be more important to people than they were 30 years ago."[87]

Or possibly, as sociologist and poet Loren Eiseley suggested years ago,[88] evolution now has shifted to the subtler levels of the human mind, with human consciousness and its drive towards expansiveness holding the key.

We, the authors, are over forty, and while writing this book we thought most of our readers would also be middle aged. We wanted to address the cynicism we've seen in many of our peers. But in retrospect, we're glad to see that anyone, of any age, who seeks the joys of companionship, can use and appreciate a little help along the way. To be true to ourselves is a universal goal, and who wouldn't want a mate who loves us for who we really are? Showing up in all our glory is the great challenge, so our strategy has not been to provide a dating manual, but to help you be ready for love and a solid relationship from the inside-out.

We believe the search for a life companion should focus more on becoming an ideal mate than on finding one. As we cultivate in ourselves the qualities and virtues we desire in a partner, we will attract people who can recognize and appreciate us and who are willing to walk alongside us on the path of authenticity.

Moving forward on this path means to continue taking emotional risks and responding in open and honest ways that leave us vulnerable. That is how trust and intimacy take root and grow.

Being real aligns us with the best in human nature and is the most direct path to genuine intimacy and personal fulfillment. It opens us to the excitement and joy of living fully in the present moment, able at last to find, nurture and keep a relationship in which we are ideal mates for each other, able to fulfill the golden promise of loving each other unconditionally for who we really are.

Sail Forth! Steer for the deep waters only,

For we are bound where mariner has not yet dared to go,

And we will risk the ship, ourselves and all.

O my brave soul! O farther, farther sail!

O daring joy, but safe!

Are they not all the seas of God?

O farther, farther, farther sail.

~ Walt Whitman "Passage to India"

ℐootnotes

CHAPTER 1. THE GIFTS OF MATURITY

1. Rilke, Ranier Maria, *Letters to a Young Poet,* Sherman Oaks, CA: New World Library, 1992.

2. Jung, Carl Gustav, *Memories, Dreams and Reflections,* New York: Vintage, 1965.

CHAPTER 2. TEN BELIEFS THAT DESTROY INTIMACY

3. Weiss, Joseph, and Sampson, Harold, *The Psychoanalytic Process,* New York: Guilford Press, 1986.

4. Weiss and Sampson, op. cit. p. 9. Presidential Task Force on Post-traumatic Stress Disorder and Trauma in Children and Adolescents, *Children and Trauma, Update for Mental Health Professionals,* 2008.

5. Weiss, and Sampson, *The Psychoanalytic Process,* op. cit., page 48.

6. American Psychological Association, 2008 Presidential Task Force on Posttraumatic Stress Disorder and Trauma in Children and Adolescents. www.apa.org/pi/families/resources/children-trauma-update.aspx

7. Clark, Aminah, *How To Raise Teenagers' Self Esteem,* Los Angeles: Price Stern Sloan, Inc., 1978.

8. Hora, Thomas, M.D., *THE SOUNDLESS MUSIC OF LIFE: Mental Liberation from Calculative Interaction and Thinking,* PAGL Foundation; Second edition, 2008. p. 26.

9. Gorski, Terrence T., *Getting Love Right: Learning the Choices of Healthy Intimacy,* Lady Lake, FL :Fireside Press, 1993, p. 29.

10. Miller, Alice, *The Drama of the Gifted Child.* New York: Basic Books, 1981; Engel, Lewis and Ferguson, Tom, *Imaginary Crimes: Why We Punish Ourselves and How to Stop.* Boston: Houghton Mifflin,1990; Bradshaw, John, Ph.D., *Healing the Shame that Binds You,* Health Communications: Deerfield Beach, Florida 1988.

11. *Newsweek,* October 1986, quoted in Faludi, Susan, *Backlash,* New York: Doubleday, 1991.

12. Faludi, Susan, *Backlash,* New York: Doubleday, 1991, pp. 11-15.

13. Page, Susan, *If I'm So Wonderful, Why Am I Still Single?,* New York: Viking, 1988; Bantam, 1991.

14. Macleish, Archibald, *The Great American Fourth of July Parade: A Verse Play for Radio,* Pittsburgh: University of Pittsburg Press, 1975.

15. Engel, Dr. Lewis, and Ferguson, Dr. Tom, *Imaginary Crimes,* New York: Houghton Mifflin, 1990.

16. Weiss and Sampson, op. cit, p. 166-167.

17. Page, op. cit. p. 101.

18. Lewis, Helen Block., *Shame and Guilt in Neurosis.* New York: International Universities Press 1971. p. 27.

19. Bradshaw, John, Ph.D., *Healing the Shame that Binds You,* Health Communications: Deerfield Beach, Florida 1988. p. vii.

20. Benedict, Ruth, "Cultural Models of Shame and Guilt" http://psych.stanford.edu/~tsailab/PDF/yw07sce.pdf.

21. Erikson, Erik, cited in *Theories of Developmental Psychology,* by Patricia H. Miller, Worth Publishers; Fifth Edition. December 22, 2009.

22. Bradshaw, *Healing the Shamethat Binds You,* revised edition, Health Communications: Deerfield Beach, Florida. 2005.

23. Bradshaw, ibid.

24. Bradshaw, op cit, p. vii.

25. Bradshaw, op. cit, p. xvii.

26. Sullivan, H.S., *The Interpersonal Theory of Psychiatry,* New York: Norton, 1953.

27. Clark, Aminah, ibid.

CHAPER 3. YOU WERE RIGHT TO WAIT

28. Foreman, Steve, "Control Mastery Theory in Relation to Attachment Theory and Mentalization-based Therapy, A Summary," San Francisco Psychotherapy Research Group Clinic and Training Center Newsletter, June 20, 2011.

29. Weiss, op. cit. p. 48.

30. Weiss, ibid.

31. Schmitz, Ashleigh, "Do 50% of Marriages Really End in Divorce?" YourTango.com, April 3 2013.

32. Popenoe, D., and Whitehead, B. D. (2007). "The state of our unions 2007: The social health of marriage in America." Piscataway, NJ: The National Marriage Project. (See pp. 18–19.) http://nationalmarriageproject.org/

CHAPTER 4. THE PATH OF AUTHENTICITY

33. Bellman, Geoff. *The Consultant's Calling,* revised edition, San Francisco: Jossey Bass, 2001, p. 70.

34. Erikson, Erik, *Childhood and Society,* New York: Norton & Co, 1963.

35. Branden, Nathaniel, *The Psychology of Romantic Love,* Los Angeles: Tarcher, 1980.

36. Drs. Masters and Johnson, quoted in Branden, op cit.

37. Keyes, Ken, *The Power of Unconditional Love,* Coos Bay, Oregon: Love Line Books, 1990.

38. Lerner, Dr. Harriet, *The Dance of Intimacy,* New York: Harper & Row, 1989.

39. *Kornfield, Jack, The Wise Heart,* New York: Random House, Bantam, 2009. p. 129.

40. Rozak, Theodore, *The Making of the Counter-Culture,* New York: Doubleday, 1969; Adorno, Theodore, *Critical Theory,* Del Mar, CA: Continuum Press, 1978.

41. Borysenko, Joan, *Minding the Body. Mending the Mind,* Boston: Addison Wesley, 1987, p. 6.

42. Wright, H. Norman, *The Premarital Counseling Handbook.* Chicago: Moody Press, 1992.

43. Lerner, Harriet, *The Dance of Anger,* New York: Harper Perennial, 2005, p. 1.

44. Lerner, op.cit. p. 1.

45. Lerner, op. cit. p. 2.

46. Lerner, ibid.

47. Greenberger, Dennis and Padesky, Christine, *Mind Over Mood,* New York, NY: The Guilford Press; 1st edition (March 15, 1995).

48. Reprinted with permission from *Inventory of Anger Communication,* by Dr. Millard J. Bienvenu Sr, Northwest Counseling Service. 710 Watson Drive, Natchitoches, Louisiana 71457, (318) 352-8345. Dr. Bienvenu has many excellent inventories and stress management materials you may write to him for.

49. Stolorow, Robert, San Francisco *San Francisco Psychotherapy Research Group and Training Center Newsletter,* October 20, 2012.

50. Weiss, Joseph, Sampson, Harold and the Mt. Zion Psychotherapy Research Group, op cit. p. 59.

51. Weiss, Sampson, op. cit. p. 60-61.

Zahn-Waxler, C. and Radke-Yarrow, M., "The development of altruism: Alternative research strategies," in *The Development of Prosocial Behavior,* ed. By N. Eisenberg, Academic Press, New York, 1982. and Gopnik, A., Meltzoff, A., and Kuhl, P. *The Scientist In the Crib, What Early Learning Tells Us about the Mind,* Perennial, New York, 2001. Cited in *San Francisco Psychotherapy Research Group and Training Center Newsletter,* June, 2013.

52. Satir, Virginia, *Conjoint Family Therapy,* Palo Alto: Science and Behavior Books, 1967. p. 2-3.

53. Satir, op. cit., p. 39.

54. Engel, Lewis and Ferguson, Tom, *Imaginary Crimes: Why We Punish Ourselves and How To Stop,* New York: Houghton Mifflin, 1990.

55. Larson, Dale, PhD., in *Family Circle Magazine,* quoted in *Marin Independent Journal,* Nov. 7, 1994.

56. Gordon, Dr. Thomas, *Parent Effectiveness Training,* New York: New American Library, 1975.

57. Albrecht, Karl, Ph.D., "The (Only) Five Basic Fears We All Live By," *Psychology Today,* March 22, 2012.

58. Schutz, Will, from a lecture at Antioch University West, San Francisco, CA, c.1983.

59. Gottman. John, *A Couple's Guide to Communication,* Champaign, Illinois: Research Press, 1976.

60. Gordon, ibid.

61. Peck, M. Scott, *The Road Less Traveled,* New York: Simon & Schuster, 1978.

62. Covey, Dr. Stephen R., *The Seven Habits of Highly Effective People,* New York: Simon & Schuster Trade, 1989.

63. Mehrabian, Albert, "Communication Without Words," *Psychology Today,* September 1968, p. 89.

64. Nierenberg, Gerald and Calero, Henry, *How to Read a Person Like a Book,* New York: Pocket Books, 1973.

65. *Holy Bible,* Book of Isaiah, 3:9.

66. Gordon, ibid.

67. Gordon, op. cit., p. 50-51.

68. Gordon, op.cit, p. 57.

69. Weiss, Joseph, "Testing Hypotheses About Unconscious Mental Functioning," *International Journal of Psychoanalysis,* 1988;69, (Pt.1): pp.87-95.

70. op. cit., pp. 12-15.

71. Gordon, ibid.

72. Farrel, Warren, *The Liberated Man,* New York: Bantam, 1974.

73. Kornfield, Jack, *A Path With Heart,* Bantam Books, 1993, p. 58.

74. Wallace, David Foster, "Commencement address to the graduates of Kenyon College in 2005." Print version: http://moreintelligentlife.com/story/david-foster-wallace-in-his-own-words. Audio version: www.youtube.com/watch?v=hJG7XcwDsuA.

75. Kornfield, ibid.

76. Kornfield, op.cit., pp. 59 and 63.

77. Cermak, Timmen, *Diagnosing and Treating Co-Dependence.* Minneapolis: Johnson Institute Books, 1986.

78. Enright, Robert D., and North, Joanna, *Exploring Forgiveness,* Madison: University of Wisconsin Press, 1998, p. 46.

79. *Yoga Journal*, #83, Nov-Dec, 1988.

80. "To Heaven and Back," CNN Special, December 1, 2013.

81. Zahn-Waxler, C. & Radke-Yarrow, M., op cit, p. 46.

82. Engel. Dr. Lewis, and Ferguson, Dr. Tom, *op.cit.*

83. Weiss and Sampson, op.cit., p. 46-47 and p. 54-55.

84. Kornfield, Jack, "Forgiveness Meditation." http://www.jackkorn-field.org/meditations/forgivenessMeditation.php.

CONCLUSION

85. Peck, op. cit.

86. Harmon, Willis, President, Institute of Noetic Sciences, San Francisco, CA.

87. Eiseley, Loren. *The Immense Journey,* New York: Vintage Books, 1957.

Bibliography

Adorno, Theodore. *Critical Theory,* Del Mar, CA: Continuum Press, 1978.

Albrecht, Karl, Ph.D., "The (Only) Five Basic Fears We All Live By," *Psychology Today,* March 22, 2012.

Barrett, Karen, PhD. 1995, 1998a. cited in ff Mills, Rosemary S.L., "Taking stock of the developmental literature on shame," Department of Family Social Sciences, University of Manitoba, Winnipeg, Manitoba, Canada R3T 2N2 revised 25 June 2004. http://sfprg.org/control_mastery/docs/shamelit.pdf

Bellman, Geoff. *The Consultant's Calling,* San Francisco: Jossey Bass, revised edition, 2001.

Benedict, Ruth, "Cultural Models of Shame and Guilt" http://psych.stanford.edu/~tsailab/PDF/yw07sce.pdf

Bienvenu, Dr. Millard J. Sr., *Inventory of Anger Communication,* Louisiana: Northwest Counseling Service.

Borysenko, Joan, *Minding the Body. Mending the Mind,* Boston: Addison Wesley, 1987.

Bradshaw, John, *Healing the Shame that Binds You,* Florida: Health Communications, Inc, 1988.

Branden, Nathaniel, *The Psychology of Romantic Love,* Los Angeles: Tarcher, 1980.

Cermak, Timmen, *Diagnosing and Treating Co-Dependence,* Minneapolis, Johnson Institute Books, 1986.

Clark, Amina, *How To Raise Teenagers' Self-Esteem,* Los Angeles, CA: Price Stern Sloan, Inc., 1980.

CNN, "To Heaven and Back," CNN Special, December 1, 2013.

Covey, Dr. Stephen R., *The Seven Habits of Highly Effective People,* Simon & Schuster Trade, New York: 1989.

Eiseley, Loren. *The Immense Journey,* New York: Vintage Books, 1957.

Engel, Dr. Lewis and Ferguson, Dr. Tom, *Imaginary Crimes,* New York: Houghton Mifflin, 1990.

Enright, Robert D., and North, Joanna, *Exploring Forgiveness,* Madison: University of Wisconsin Press, 1998.

Erikson, Erik, *Childhood and Society,* New York: Norton & Co, 1963.

Faludi, Susan, *Backlash,* New York: Doubleday, 1991.

Farrel, Warren, *The Liberated Man,* New York: Bantam, 1974.

Gordon, Dr. Thomas, *Parent Effectiveness Training,* New York: New American Library, 1975.

Gorski, Terrence T., *Getting Love Right: Learning the Choices of Healthy Intimacy,* Lady Lake, FL :Fireside Press, 1993.

Gottman. John, *A Couple's Guide to Communication,* Champaign, Illinois: Research Press, 1976.

Greenberger, Dennis and Padesky, Christine, *Mind Over Mood,* New York, NY: The Guilford Press; 1st edition (March 15, 1995.

Harmon, Willis, President, Institute of Noetic Sciences, San Francisco, CA.

Holy Bible, Book of Isaiah, 3:9.

Hora, Thomas, M.D., *THE SOUNDLESS MUSIC OF LIFE: Mental Liberation from Calculative and Interaction and Thinking,* PAGL Foundation; Second edition (May 1, 2008).

Jung, Carl Gustav, *Memories, Dreams and Reflections,* New York: Vintage, 1965.

Keyes, Ken, *The Power of Unconditional Love,* Coos Bay, Oregon: 1990.

Kornfield, Jack, *A Path With Heart,* New York: Random House, Bantam Books, 1993.

Kornfield, Jack, *The Wise Heart: A Guide to the Universal Teachings of Buddhist Psychology,* New York: Random House, Bantam Books, 2009.

Larson, Dale, PhD., in *Family Circle Magazine,* quoted in *Marin Independent Journal,* Nov. 7, 1994.

Lerner, Harriet, *The Dance of Anger,* New York: Harper Perennial, 2005.

_____ *The Dance of Intimacy,* New York: Harper & Row, 1989.

Macleish, Archibald, *The Great American Fourth of July Parade: A Verse Play for Radio,* Pittsburgh: University of Pittsburg Press, 1975.

Mehrabian, Albert, "Communication Without Words," *Psychology Today,* Sept. 1968.

Miller, Alice, *The Drama of the Gifted Child.* New York: Basic Books, 1981.

Miller, Patricia H., *Theories of Developmental Psychology.* New York: Worth Publishers; Fifth Edition, 2009.

Newsweek, October 1986, quoted in Faludi, Susan, *Backlash,* New York: Doubleday, 1991.

Nierenberg, Gerald and Calero, Henry, *How to Read a Person Like a Book,* New York: Pocket Books, 1973.

Page, Susan, *If I'm So Wonderful, Why Am I Still Single?,* New York: Viking, 1988; Bantam, 1991.

Peck, M. Scott, *The Road Less Traveled,* New York: Simon & Schuster, 1978.

Popenoe, D., and Whitehead, B. D. (2007). "The state of our unions 2007: The social health of marriage in America." Piscataway, NJ: The National Marriage Project. (See pp. 18–19.) http://nationalmarriageproject.org/

Presidential Task Force on Posttraumatic Stress Disorder and

Trauma in Children and Adolescents, *Children and Trauma, Update for Mental Health Professionals,* 2008.

Rilke, Ranier Maria, *Letters to a Young Poet,* Sherman Oaks, CA: New World Library, 1992.

Rozak, Theodore, *The Making of the Counter-Culture,* New York: Doubleday, 1969.

Satir, Virginia, *Conjoint Family Therapy,* Palo Alto: Science and Behavior Books, 1967.

Schmitz, Ashleigh, "Do 50% of Marriages Really End in Divorce?" YourTango.com, April 3 2013.

Schutz, Will, from a lecture at Antioch University West, San Francisco, CA, c.1983.

Smith, Dr. Michael H., "Forgiveness: A New Paradigm for Diversity Training," *Vision/Action, The Journal of the Bay Area Organization Development Network,* Volume 12, #2, Summer 1993. pp. 1-4.

Stolorow, Robert, *San Francisco Psychotherapy Research Group Newsletter,* October 20, 2012.

Sullivan, H.S., *The Interpersonal Theory of Psychiatry,* New York: Norton, 1953.

Wallace, David Foster, "Commencement address to the graduates of Kenyon College in 2005." Print version: http://moreintelligentlife.com/story/david-foster-wallace-in-his-own-words. Audio version: http://www.youtube.com/watch?v=hJG7XcwDsuA.

Weiss, Joseph, and Sampson, Harold, and the Mt. Zion Psychotherapy Research Group, *The Psychoanalytic Process,* New York: Guilford Press, 1986.

Weiss, Joseph & Sampson, Harold, *"The Psychoanalytic Process,"* p. 92 -ff; in *Empirical studies of psychoanalytic theories,"* Vol. 8. Washington, DC: *American Psychological Association,* xxxiv, 321 pp. doi: 10.1037/10275-009.

Weiss, Joseph, "Testing Hypotheses About Unconscious Mental Functioning," *International Journal of Psychoanalysis,* 1988;69, (Pt.1).

_____, "Unconscious Mental Functioning," *Scientific American,* March, 1990.

_____, *How Psychotherapy Works, Process and Technique,* 1993, pp. 4-5.

Wright, H. Norman, *The Premarital Counseling Handbook.* Chicago: Moody Press, 1992.

Yoga Journal, #83, Nov-Dec, 1988.

Zahn-Waxler, C. and Radke-Yarrow, M., "The Development of Altruism: Alternative Research Strategies," in *The Development of Prosocial Behavior,* ed. by N. Eisenberg, Academic Press, New York, 1982 and Gopnik, A., Meltzoff, A. & Kuhl, P. *The Scientist In the Crib, What Early Learning Tells Us About the Mind,* New York: Perennial, 2001.

About the Authors

Karen McChrystal, M.A., MFCC, is an author and interdisciplinary researcher. She is the Publisher and Editor-in-Chief for Quantum Era Press, based in Santa Monica, California, which provides all prepress services to independent authors. As well, she is the Executive Director and a founder of the Sustainable Living Institute, a non-profit organization based in Santa Monica, California.

Her undergraduate studies were done at Stanford University, where she received a BA in political science. She completed a Master's degree in Clinical Psychology at the Western Institute for Social Research, in San Francisco, California.

After graduating with a BA, she worked as an investigative journalist and was an editor/managing editor for various print publications. After receiving her Master's degree and MFCC license, she had a successful private practice as a psychotherapist for thirteen years, then quit to be able to do something different – first to pursue environmentalism, then to work in the Internet industry as editor for online publications. For the past twelve years, as owner of Quantum Era Press, she has been helping other authors publish their own books.

She is also the author of *Garden of Light: Aligning with Your True Nature and Receiving Inner Guidance* (Warm Springs Press, 2016), *The Creative Process* (Warm Springs Press, 1980, 2016), *A Committed Spiritual Life: The Royal Road to Self-Evolution* (Warm Springs Press, 2016. ebook), *The Breath of Life: A Path to Inner Peace* (Warm Springs Press, 2016. ebook), a volume of poetry, *Letting the Wind Blow* (Warm Springs Press, 2016. ebook), and *The Breath of Life: Stress Management Plus,* by Karen McChrystal and Steven L. Ross (1998, audiocassette).

Contact information:
• kmcchrystal@gmail.com

* * *

Steven L. Ross, M.A., LMFT, graduated from Stanford University with a BA in English Literature and a minor in Psychology. Soon after that he took monastic vows and taught yoga and meditation for nearly a decade abroad. Returning home, he earned a Master's degree in Clinical Psychology from Antioch University West. He was licensed in California as a Marriage and Family

Therapist in 1990 and maintained a private practice in the San Francisco Bay Area until moving to Arizona in 2002. He currently maintains a counseling and wellness practice in Tucson, Mindful Counseling & Consulting, specializing in stress management and anxiety reduction. He facilitates a University-based men's cancer support group and regularly teaches mindfulness meditation classes in the tradition of Theravada Buddhism.

Contact information:
• steve.ross@breathingcoachtucson.com, (520) 825-2009, or
• www.relaxandbreathe.net.

www.ingramcontent.com/pod-product-compliance
Lightning Source LLC
Chambersburg PA
CBHW070951040426
42443CB00007B/456